# THE NORTH KOREAN THREAT: NUCLEAR, MISSILES AND CYBER

## BRIEFING

BEFORE THE

## COMMITTEE ON FOREIGN AFFAIRS
## HOUSE OF REPRESENTATIVES

ONE HUNDRED FOURTEENTH CONGRESS

FIRST SESSION

JANUARY 13, 2015

Serial No. 114–2

Printed for the use of the Committee on Foreign Affairs

Available via the World Wide Web: http://www.foreignaffairs.house.gov/ or
http://www.gpo.gov/fdsys/

U.S. GOVERNMENT PUBLISHING OFFICE

92–556PDF                WASHINGTON : 2015

(II)

# CONTENTS

# THE NORTH KOREAN THREAT: NUCLEAR, MISSILES AND CYBER

## TUESDAY, JANUARY 13, 2015

HOUSE OF REPRESENTATIVES,
COMMITTEE ON FOREIGN AFFAIRS,
*Washington, DC.*

The briefing was held, pursuant to notice, at 10:10 a.m., in room 2172, Rayburn House Office Building, Hon. Ed Royce (chairman of the committee) presiding.

Chairman ROYCE. This briefing will come to order.

As the members here know, we are not going to be able to formally organize until next week, but I very much appreciate the ranking member, Mr. Engel, his cooperation in beginning this process of holding today a briefing so that we can get started on the many pressing issues that we face, and I look forward to meeting next week to formally organize the committee and discuss how all of us can work together in a bipartisan way in order to advance U.S. interests around the world.

And one of the things I have enjoyed about working with this committee is the way Mr. Engel and myself and the members here on the committee have been able to advance the idea that we work on a consensus and then move that forward with one voice overseas, and I think that amplifies the message from the United States.

But the issue that we are discussing today, North Korea, is one where for years the United States and our allies have been rightly concerned about the threat from North Korea's nuclear missile programs.

Mr. Sherman and myself remember very vividly the situation of proliferation by North Korea with respect to the transfer of that capability into Syria and, on the banks of the Euphrates, a weapons program being developed there as a consequence of North Korea, and for years we have watched that program grow.

And now this brutal regime has added a new weapon to its arsenal, which is cyberattacks, and the state-sanctioned cyber attack on Sony pictures underscored three unchanging facts about North Korea: First, this rogue regime has no interest in being a responsible state.

Second, while Kim Jong Un continues to carry out human rights abuses around the world and by carrying out attacks, for those of you who remember some of the exercises that the North Koreans have taken offshore, as well, most importantly, of what they have done to their own people.

(1)

The way in which a country treats its own people will sometimes tell us how they will treat others. The current President of South Korea, her mother was assassinated by North Korean agents.

So, we looked at that U.N. report that was recently filed, after the evidence and interviews with many of the survivors, defectors out of North Korea, this was the conclusion of the report. The United Nations has found no parallel in the contemporary world for the treatment of people in North Korea. That is quite a statement.

And in the meantime, of course, instead of assisting that population, the resources that North Korea gets its hands on continues to go into its nuclear and missile systems and, of course, cyber weapon capability as well.

And third, the third point, North Korea's weapons are not merely for show. We and our allies in Northeast Asia are facing a brutal and dangerous regime, one that not only is trying to miniaturize nuclear weapons to put them on ICBM's, but also one, as I said earlier, that has been involved in the past in central Asia and in the Middle East in proliferating these different types of weapons, missiles and other types of offensive capabilities as well as nuclear weapons capability.

So North Korea's growing cyber capability emerged most starkly in 2013. Our ally, South Korea, suffered a series of cyberattacks that temporarily brought down some of the commercial and media networks, it disrupted banking systems. The hackers called this Dark Soul, but in particular what they were able to do was to shut down the banking systems in parts of the country, shut down the ATM systems and so forth.

Despite limited internet capability in North Korea, the fact is that there is an elite cyber ware warfare unit the defectors have told us about, Bureau 121, which was traced back as the source of these attacks on South Korea. And some of the expertise was obtained overseas by sending them to other countries for training, but certainly that capability was deployed against South Korea.

And last year's cyber attack is estimated to have cost Sony hundreds of millions of dollars in damage. It was a state-sanctioned attack that has many Americans asking, ''If that is what North Korea can do to a movie company, how vulnerable is our critical infrastructure, how vulnerable is our electric grid?'' You know, what if electricity was cut off? I mean, that obviously could be a dark chapter.

Earlier this month the administration announced long overdue sanctions targeting officials and front companies of the North Korean Government. And I am glad the administration has described this as just the first aspect of its response, because many of those individuals who were blacklisted had already been targeted by U.S. sanctions.

But the significance of this new Executive order may come from the broad power it gives the President to target anyone who is a part of the North Korean Government or is assisting them in any way, that is, if the administration chooses to use it to its full advantage.

We need to step up and target those financial institutions in Asia and beyond that are supporting the brutal and dangerous North Korean regime. Such sanctions have crippled North Korea in the past. For those of us who remember the consequences on Banco Delta Asia being sanctioned, and left the regime unable to buy the loyalties of its generals at that time, who could not be paid.

This committee has been focused on the North Korea threat for years, bringing attention to the regime's human rights abuses, its illicit criminal activities, its growing nuclear and missile programs, and helpful scrutiny of North Korean nuclear negotiations.

Indeed, last Congress the House passed legislation that Ranking Member Eliot Engel and I authored to ramp up the financial pressure on North Korea, pressing for North Korea to be designated a primary money laundering concern, as has been done with Iran, curtailing its sale of weapons and stepping up inspections of North Korean ships, among other steps. Unfortunately, the Senate failed to act on this critical legislation before it adjourned, but we will soon try again and give the Senate a chance to join us in tackling this growing threat.

And I will now turn to the ranking member for his opening comments.

Mr. ENGEL. Thank you very much, Chairman Royce.

Thank you for calling this briefing on the threat that North Korea's nuclear missile and cyber capabilities pose to our national security and that of our friends and allies in the Asia Pacific region.

I want to on a personal note say that I commend your strong leadership on this issue, and it means a great deal that this briefing is the very first item on our committee's agenda in the 114th Congress.

I look forward to working with you and the rest of our colleagues to address this challenge and to continue working in a bipartisan and productive way in the year ahead, and I want to second what you said. It is very important for us, whenever possible, to have one voice in international affairs. It strengthens us, it strengthens us around the world, and that is what we have tried to do in this committee.

So you and I, Mr. Chairman, have introduced joint legislation, we have written joint pieces, joint op ed pieces, we have done joint letters to officials, and I believe that we have gotten the biggest bang for the buck because we have shown unity on this committee.

One of the things that I have noticed is when I go overseas and we take a bipartisan delegation along, our differences really, really narrow, because we are all Americans and we all love this country, and I think it is very important. I think this committee leads the way in terms of the way Congress ought to govern in a bipartisan fashion.

So I want to thank you, Mr. Chairman, for all you do to ensure that that continues.

I also want to thank our witnesses for their service and for their testimony today.

The recalcitrance, cruelty, and unpredictability of the Kim regime makes North Korea one of the toughest challenges we face on the global stage. The last three administrations, Democratic and Republican alike, have attempted to address the problem of North Korea's nuclear program. Unfortunately, very little progress has been made. Despite a long list of sanctions, North Korea is no closer to denuclearization today than it was several decades ago; rather, North Korea has continued to develop its nuclear, conventional and cyber capabilities at an alarming rate.

Already North Korea has a significant arsenal of short-range missiles that could reach South Korea and Japan. Most troubling to me is the continued development of North Korea's medium and long-range missile capabilities. They may be unreliable today, but some of these missiles could eventually pose a threat to Guam, Alaska or even the west coast of the continental United States. And some believe that North Korea has aspirations to build submarines that could carry these missiles even closer to American shores.

North Korea appears to be working toward a miniaturized nuclear warhead that could be mounted on intermediate and long-range missiles. I was concerned by comments made in October by the commander of U.S. forces in Korea that at this moment, North Korea may possess the ability to miniaturize a nuclear warhead.

And based on recent events, it is clear that North Korea's aspirations do not stop at conventional or even nuclear weapons. The Kim regime is wielding 21st century weapons as well, and has quietly developed an offensive cyber capability.

Like many others, I was deeply disturbed by the cyber attack on Sony that took place in November, an attack that was not just disruptive, but also destructive. Agents working for the North Korea regime vandalized, threatened and coerced a company operating in the United States. This attack and the ensuing threats of violence were a perverse and inexcusable act by the North Korean Government.

As I said then, no one, especially an entity operating in the United States, should feel that they must cede their rights to operate within the law because of veiled threats from rogue actors.

I look forward to the witnesses, to hearing how each of your departments is dealing with this threat, are you engaging with the private sector? Are you ramping up information sharing and collaboration across agencies? Are you putting safeguards in place to ensure that these kinds of attacks will not be successful in the future? I look forward to hearing about your progress in these areas.

There is no international agreement or clear definition of what constitutes cyber war or cyber terror, yet, it is clear that cyberattacks can cause destruction of property, stoke fear, intimidate the public, or even bring about the loss of life that could be as serious as conventional acts of war or terrorism.

We must assure that North Korea's cyber capabilities and the cyber capabilities of other state-sponsored and rogue actors do not threaten our citizens, our businesses, or our national security. I would like to hear the witnesses' assessments of these risks and our ability and the ability of allies and partners to effectively defend against them.

Finally, let's remember that the greatest threat the regime in Pyongyang poses is to its own people. I have visited North Korea twice myself—Mr. Wilson of this committee was with me on one of the trips—and I still remember the incredible uneasiness that I felt being in a place where absolute power is consolidated among a very few and where the rest of society is systematically and brutally oppressed.

For years we have heard reports about the abuses endured by the people of North Korea, torture, starvation, forced labor and execution. A recent United Nations Commission of Inquiry report confirmed these reports, calling the North Korean regime responsible for systematic, widespread, and gross human rights violations, including what they said was crimes against humanity.

The chairman and I share a deep commitment to addressing the injustices endured by the North Korean people. So we face a delicate balance: Holding the Korean leaders who perpetuate this violence accountable while recognizing the need for basic support for the North Korean people. Maintaining that balance makes our work on North Korea all the more critical and all the more difficult.

So I look forward to hearing your perspectives on this issue, and I thank you for joining us today.

Thank you, Mr. Chairman.

Chairman ROYCE. Thank you, Mr. Engel.

This morning we are joined by representatives from the Department of State, from Treasury and from Homeland Security.

Ambassador Sung Kim is the Special Representative for the North Korea Policy and the Deputy Assistant Secretary for Korea and Japan. Previously he served as U.S. Ambassador to the Republic of Korea and he was the special envoy for the Six-Party Talks.

Honorable Daniel Glaser, prior to his confirmation as Assistant Secretary for Terrorist Finance in the Office of Terrorism and Financial Intelligence at the Department of Treasury, he served as the first director of the Treasury's Executive Office of Terrorist Financing and Financial Crimes.

Brigadier General Gregory Touhill is Deputy Assistant Secretary for Cybersecurity Operations and Programs at the Department of Homeland Security. Previously he served in the United States Air Force as the Chief Information Officer and Director of Command Control Communications and Cybersystems at U.S. Transportation Command.

And so without objection, the briefer's full prepared statement will be made part of the record here, members will have 5 calendar days to submit any statements to you or questions or put any extraneous material into the record.

And, Ambassador Kim, if you would like to begin. And if you could summarize your remarks, and then we will go to questions.

## STATEMENT OF THE HONORABLE SUNG KIM, SPECIAL REPRESENTATIVE FOR NORTH KOREA POLICY AND DEPUTY ASSISTANT SECRETARY FOR KOREA AND JAPAN, U.S. DEPARTMENT OF STATE

Ambassador KIM. Thank you very much, Mr. Chairman, Ranking Member Engel and members of the committee.

Thank you very much for inviting me today along with my colleagues from Treasury and Homeland Security to testify about North Korea.

As we respond to North Korea's destabilizing, provocative and repressive policies and actions, we appreciate the interest and attention you and the committee have given to this important issue.

In recent weeks, Mr. Chairman, the American people and the international community have been deeply troubled by the destructive cyber attack on Sony Pictures Entertainment. An extensive FBI investigation has concluded that the attack was conducted by the Government of North Korea.

The administration is totally committed to defending U.S. citizens, U.S. businesses, and our Nation's constitutionally-protected right of free speech. That is why the President made clear that the United States would respond proportionally to the DPRK's attack in a time and a manner of our choosing.

Our response to the attack on Sony is consistent with our policy on the DPRK across the board, one which seeks to work with our allies and partners to increase the cost to North Korea of its irresponsible behavior, to sharpen the regime's choices, and to persuade the DPRK peacefully to abandon its nuclear weapons program, respect the human rights of its people, and abide by international norms and obligations.

Mr. Chairman, as you stated eloquently in a recent interview, we need to change the equilibrium in North Korea and move the regime away from hostility. Together with the international community, we are using the full range of tools at our disposal to make clear to the DPRK that abandoning its nuclear weapons, provocative actions and human rights abuses is the only way to end the political and economic isolation.

In our messages to the DPRK and to our partners, we have made clear that we will respond to the DPRK's misbehavior. The Executive order signed by the President on January 2nd is an important new tool. It responds to the attack on Sony Pictures, but also provides a framework for addressing the full range of DPRK illicit behavior.

In applying this pressure, just as in our efforts at engagement, our work with our allies is vital. The United States has very limited economic and other ties with the DPRK, so our financial sanctions are much more effective when supported by our partners.

We also work with our allies to deter DPRK aggression. Having left Seoul as Ambassador just a few months ago, I can tell you that our alliance with South Korea is stronger than ever, and our growing trilateral security cooperation with South Korea and Japan also sends a powerful message of deterrence to Pyongyang.

If I may Mr. Chairman, I would like to take this opportunity to thank you and the committee for the committee's strong support for our robust alliances with both Japan and South Korea.

Mr. Chairman, as we apply unilateral and multilateral pressure and strengthen our deterrence, we will continue our principal diplomacy. We have made clear to the DPRK that the door is open to meaningful engagement. Close coordination with our partners in the Six-Party process is essential. Thanks to our continued robust engagement with South Korea, Japan, China and Russia, our unity has never been stronger. Wherever Pyongyang turns, it hears a strong, unwavering message from all five parties echoed by the wider international community that it will not be accepted as a nuclear power.

Our alliances with Japan and the Republic of Korea are a bedrock of our Six-Party diplomacy. Both allies are resolute and their commitment in their goal of the denuclearization of the Korean peninsula and the end to North Korea's illicit behavior. Both governments have condemned the attack on Sony Pictures and express solidarity with the United States in our response.

To intensify our coordination, I will travel to Tokyo for trilateral talks with my Japanese and South Korean counterparts later this month. On that trip, I will also visit Beijing to strengthen our cooperation with China.

China has done a great deal on North Korea. We believe it can do more. In the wake of the cyber attack against Sony Pictures, China did condemn malicious behavior in cyberspace.

Although Russia has recently pursued investment in North Korea and invited Kim Jong Un to visit Moscow later this year, our alignment on the core goal of denuclearization remains strong as ever.

We also work actively with partners in the broader international community, especially on human rights. Building on the important work of the U.N. Commission of Inquiry, this past year the U.N. Human Rights Commission and General Assembly adopted by overwhelming margins resolutions calling for accountability for North Korea's human rights abuses. Just last month, the U.N. Security Council took up the DPRK's grave human rights injustices on their standing agenda for the very first time.

Mr. Chairman, standing up to North Korea requires a sustained and concerted effort by all of the countries in the Six-Party process and indeed by the entire international community. Together, we will, to borrow your words again, ''change the equilibrium in North Korea and persuade Pyongyang that North Korea will not achieve security or economic prosperity while pursuing nuclear weapons, trampling on international norms, and abusing its own people.''

Thank you again for the opportunity to appear before this committee.

Chairman ROYCE. Thank you, Ambassador Kim.

[The prepared statement of Ambassador Kim follows:]

**Testimony before the House Foreign Affairs Committee**

**January 13, 2014**

**Special Representative for North Korea Policy and**

**Deputy Assistant Secretary of State Sung Y. Kim**

Mr. Chairman, Ranking Member Engel, and Members of the Committee, thank you for inviting me today, along with my colleagues from Treasury and DHS, to testify about North Korea. I particularly appreciate your convening this hearing early as the new Congress begins its work. North Korea is one of the most difficult and complicated challenges the United States faces. As we respond to its destabilizing, provocative, and repressive policies and actions around the world, we appreciate the interest and attention you and the Committee have given to this issue.

**DPRK Behavior**

In recent weeks, Mr. Chairman, the American people and international community have been deeply troubled by the destructive and coercive cyber attack on Sony Pictures Entertainment, and the subsequent threats of violence against American movie theaters and moviegoers. An extensive FBI investigation has concluded that this attack was conducted by the government of the Democratic People's Republic of Korea. The Administration is totally committed to defending U.S. citizens, U.S. businesses, and our nation's constitutionally protected right of free speech. That is why the President made clear that the United States would respond proportionally to the DPRK's attack on Sony Pictures, in a time and a manner of our choosing.

Our response includes, as a first step, the Executive Order the President signed on January 2, which authorizes additional sanctions on designated agencies and officials of the DPRK government and Korean Worker's Party. My colleagues and I want to talk more about these specific measures, but I also want to make clear that our response to the attack on Sony is consistent with our policy on the DPRK across the board – one which seeks to work with our allies and partners to increase the cost to North Korea of its irresponsible behavior, to sharpen the regime's choices, and to persuade the DPRK peacefully to abandon its illicit nuclear weapons programs, respect the human rights of its people, and abide by international norms and obligations.

Sadly, the cyber attack on Sony is nothing new for the DPRK. Its destructive, destabilizing, and repressive policies range from its ongoing violations of the UN Security Council resolutions covering its nuclear and missile programs, to its deplorable human rights conditions which the United Nations has strongly condemned. In the months before the Sony attack, the DPRK launched a series of ballistic missiles in violation of multiple UN Security Council resolutions; its Ocean Maritime Management Shipping Company was sanctioned by the Security Council for its illicit proliferation of weapons around the world; and it threatened a fourth nuclear test in response to a UN General Assembly resolution which condemned the gross, widespread, and systematic human rights abuses meticulously documented in a report by a UN Commission of Inquiry.

Together with the international community, we are using the full range of tools at our disposal to make clear to the DPRK that abandoning this course and abiding by international laws and obligations is the only way to end its political and economic isolation.

**Diplomacy**

Mr. Chairman, at the center of our efforts is our persistent, principled diplomacy with our partners in northeast Asia and around the world. The United States has offered – and continues to offer – Pyongyang an improved bilateral relationship provided it takes action to demonstrate a willingness to fulfill its denuclearization commitments and address other important concerns which are also shared by the international community. We seek credible and authentic negotiations to bring the DPRK into compliance with its denuclearization obligations. We have made clear to the DPRK that the door is open to meaningful engagement, while applying unilateral and multilateral pressure to steer it toward that door. Unfortunately, while North Korea claims to seek talks without preconditions, it has consistently rebuffed or ignored our offers for dialogue and instead responded with a series of provocations – from last summer's ballistic missile launches to November's attack on Sony. We know we must judge the DPRK by its actions, not its words. We remain open to engagement when possible, but we will continue to apply pressure as needed.

**Six-Party Diplomacy**

Close coordination with North Korea's neighbors, our partners in the Six-Party Talks – the Republic of Korea, Japan, China, and Russia – is essential. While the Six-Party Talks process has regrettably been dormant since the DPRK walked out and declared the process "dead" in 2008, our continued robust engagement with the other four parties has ensured that five-party unity has never been stronger on the common goal of the verifiable denuclearization of the Korean Peninsula. This unity ensures that wherever Pyongyang turns, it hears a strong, unwavering message from all five parties – echoed by the wider international community – that it will not be accepted as a nuclear power, that it must live up to its international obligations, and that authentic and credible negotiations must be marked by concrete denuclearization steps. None of us insists that North Korea denuclearize *before* returning to the negotiating table. But we *all* refuse to be drawn into talks for the sake of talks. We have underscored the need for an early and demonstrable commitment from the DPRK to denuclearize. Instead, the DPRK has chosen to continue flouting the standards and obligations of the international community.

## ROK and Japan

Our alliances with Japan and the Republic of Korea are a bedrock of our Six-Party diplomacy. The President and Secretary Kerry speak regularly with their counterparts in Tokyo and Seoul, and this month I will travel to Japan for trilateral talks on North Korea with my South Korean and Japanese colleagues. The visit will mark my second trip to the region since assuming my current position just two months ago. Both allies are resolute in their commitment to the goal of the denuclearization of the Korean Peninsula and an end to North Korea's illicit behavior.

Our coordination has ensured that as South Korean President Park Geun-hye seeks to test Pyongyang's professed interest in improving North-South ties and healing the wounds that have divided Korean families for 70 years, there is no daylight between Washington and Seoul on what we expect from North Korea. President Park has made clear that major improvements in inter-Korean relations can come only with denuclearization, and we hope the North will embrace her principled vision. Similarly, as Japanese Prime Minister Shinzo Abe seeks the return of innocent Japanese citizens abducted by the DPRK and held for decades, Tokyo has made clear that real progress in the bilateral relationship comes only with denuclearization. In the weeks since establishing that the attack on Sony Pictures was launched by the DPRK, we have been in constant touch with both Japan and South Korea, and both governments have condemned the attack and expressed solidarity with the United States in our response.

**China**

On my upcoming trip to Northeast Asia, I will also visit Beijing. China has a unique and important role to play in addressing the challenges of North Korea's nuclear program and its provocations on the world stage. We believe there is more that China can do to bring the necessary pressure to bear so that North Korea concludes it has no choice but to denuclearize and abide by its international obligations. China has already done a great deal, and North Korea remains at the top of our bilateral agenda with China and featured prominently in the President's discussions with Xi Jinping in Beijing last November. In their meeting, both leaders affirmed that North Korea cannot succeed in pursuing both nuclear weapons and economic development. It cannot have both. In the wake of the cyber attack against Sony Pictures, China has again sent a signal to its neighbor, condemning this type of malicious behavior in cyberspace.

**Russia**

As our global cooperation with Moscow has been strained by Russia's aggression in Ukraine, the DPRK has sought to reduce its economic dependence on China by pursuing stronger ties with Russia, and Russia has responded positively. Moscow has forgiven some of the DPRK's debt, pursued investment in North Korea's railroad network, and even invited Kim Jong Un to visit Moscow later this year But our alignment on the core goal of denuclearization remains as strong as ever. When senior Russian leaders have met with their North Korean counterparts, they have consistently delivered a tough message on denuclearization. As a major stakeholder in the international nonproliferation regime, Russia will remain an important player in our diplomacy with the DPRK.

**International Community**

We also work actively with partners in the broader international community to reinforce to North Korea that its isolation will continue until its provocations cease. In the United Nations Security Council, we successfully led the charge to sanction the DPRK's major international shipping firm for its role in the regime's illicit arms trade. We have worked with partners from Australia to Southeast Asia to Africa to increase enforcement of UN sanctions and reduce the revenues the DPRK can funnel to its nuclear and missile programs.

In the months since a UN Commission of Inquiry documented in disturbing detail North Korea's dire human rights situation, we have worked closely with countries around the world to maintain attention on this issue. The UN Human Rights Council and General Assembly this past year adopted by overwhelming margins resolutions calling for accountability for North Korea's human rights abuses. For the first time just last month, the DPRK's grave human rights situation was taken up as a standing agenda item by the UN Security Council. This helps ensure continued Council attention on the egregious human rights situation in the North, and it reflects the international community's concerns for the threat to international peace and security that these systematic and widespread violations represent.

Our coordination with partners in Asia and Europe helped ensure that when North Korea's foreign minister and party secretary traveled abroad on an attempted charm offensive last fall, they heard a chorus of calls for progress on human rights and denuclearization. And in recent weeks, our international partners have joined us in condemning the destructive and coercive cyber attack on Sony Pictures, in calling on the DPRK to cease such attacks, and in supporting a proportionate response.

**Pressure**

And, in our messages to the DPRK and to our partners around the world, we have made clear that we *will* respond to the DPRK's misbehavior. We are under no illusions about the DPRK's willingness to abandon its illicit weapons, provocations, and human rights abuses on its own. We will apply pressure both multilaterally and unilaterally to increase the costs to the DPRK of its destructive policy choices.

**The New Executive Order**

The Executive Order signed by the President on January 2 is an important new tool, enhancing our ability to apply pressure on Pyongyang. It responds to the attack on Sony Pictures, but also provides a framework for addressing the full range of DPRK illicit behavior going forward. In this initial tranche of sanctions issued under the Executive Order, our application of this Executive Order has been targeted. We seek to impose consequences on the wrongdoers in the DPRK regime, not on the North Korean people. We have designated the Reconnaissance General Bureau, the DPRK's elite intelligence agency known to be responsible for many of its cyber operations, as well as its major arms dealer and missile technology procurement agency, and several of its overseas arms trade representatives.

Designating these entities and individuals under this new Executive Order, in addition to their previous designations under nonproliferation-related authorities, not only highlights the DPRK's violations of international norms and laws at a moment when the world's eyes are on Pyongyang, but also – as my colleague from Treasury can discuss in greater detail – gives us the ability in the future to designate those who provide material support to these designees. This Executive

Order is one aspect of our response to the cyber attack on Sony Pictures. My colleague from the Department of Homeland Security can elaborate on the measures the Administration is taking to shore up the cyber defenses for both the public and private sectors here at home.

## Multilateral Cooperation on Sanctions

With this expansion of sanctions, as with our existing sanctions authorities targeting the DPRK, we seek to increase the costs of North Korea's misbehavior, reduce the revenues the DPRK is able to funnel to its illicit nuclear and ballistic missile programs, and sharpen the regime's choices.

In applying this pressure, just as in our efforts at engagement, our work with allies is critical. As I mentioned, we worked together with China, Russia, and other members of the UN Security Council to designate under UN sanctions North Korea's Ocean Maritime Management shipping company, and we regularly work together with partners like Japan, South Korea, and Australia to improve sanctions implementation. We are currently briefing our partners on the authorities provided under the President's latest Executive Order, as they continuously review their own sanctions programs. This approach – balancing the need to respond decisively to

North Korea's provocations with the need to enlist support from our allies and partners – is critical to the success of our sanctions regime. The United States has very limited economic and other ties with the DPRK, hence, our financial sanctions are always more effective when supported by and – when possible – implemented together with our partners.

**Deterrence**

We also work with our allies to deter DPRK aggression. Having left Seoul as ambassador just a few months ago, I can tell you that our alliance with South Korea is stronger than ever. From our day-to-day combined efforts to maintain peace and stability on the Peninsula through our Combined Forces Command, to the counter-provocation and counter-missile planning our Department of Defense and Joint Staff colleagues engage in with their South Korean counterparts, we send a strong message to North Korea that security is not to be found in nuclear weapons and military provocations.

Our growing trilateral security cooperation with South Korea and Japan also sends a powerful message of deterrence to Pyongyang. This was seen over the last year in our trilateral Search and Rescue Exercises, our July Chiefs of Defense meeting between Chairman of the Joint Chiefs Dempsey and his counterparts in Seoul and Tokyo, the June trilateral defense ministerial meeting led by Secretary Hagel, and my own periodic discussions with my Korean and Japanese counterparts. Other measures we have taken in the region to strengthen bilateral and trilateral missile defense cooperation are also tied to our larger diplomatic strategy of building and maintaining a strong diplomatic consensus against a nuclear-armed North Korea. This past December we concluded a trilateral arrangement between the United States, the ROK, and Japan which will enable the defense authorities of our three countries to share information on the nuclear and missile threats posed by North Korea.

**Conclusion**

Ultimately, Mr. Chairman, our policy aims to bring the DPRK to the realization that it must take the steps necessary to end its isolation, respect the human rights of its own people, honor its past commitments, and comply with its international obligations.

North Korea is not, as they claim, developing nuclear weapons and intercontinental ballistic missiles in response to a threat from the United States or any outside power. Rather, North Korea believes these programs will help prolong the Kim regime and obtain material and political benefits from the international community. By portraying the United States as a strategic enemy, the DPRK hopes to strengthen its narrative that the U.S. is responsible for North Korea's bad behavior and, therefore, solely responsible for mitigating it. We are not. North Korea is responsible for North Korean actions. Standing up to North Korea requires a sustained and concerted effort by all of the countries in the Six-Party process, and indeed by the entire international community.

The leadership in Pyongyang faces ever-sharper choices. Its isolation grows with every outrageous act it commits. North Korea will not achieve security, economic prosperity, and integration into the international community while pursuing nuclear weapons, trampling on international norms, abusing its own people, and using cyberspace to destroy the property of private businesses and threaten violence on Americans.

Thank you again for the opportunity to appear before you today. I am happy to answer any questions you may have.

————————

Chairman ROYCE. Dan?

**STATEMENT OF THE HONORABLE DANIEL GLASER, ASSIST-
ANT SECRETARY FOR TERRORIST FINANCING, OFFICE OF
TERRORISM AND FINANCIAL INTELLIGENCE, U.S. DEPART-
MENT OF THE TREASURY**

Mr. GLASER. Thank you, Chairman Royce, Ranking Member
Engel, and distinguished members of this committee.

Thank you for inviting me to speak today about the U.S. Government's efforts to counter the threat posed by the malicious
cyberattacks of the DPRK.

The DPRK is a brazen and isolated regime that has repeatedly
shown flagrant disregard for international standards. This is evident in the DPRK's development and proliferation of its illicit nuclear and ballistic missile programs, its repeated violations of U.N.
Security Council resolutions, its repression of its people through serious human rights abuses, and most recently its cyber attack on
a U.S. company in attempts to stifle freedom of expression in our
country.

In response to the DPRK's cyber attack on Sony Pictures, the
President signed an Executive order, Executive Order 13687, on
January 6th, 2015, granting the Treasury Department the author-
ity to impose sanctions against agencies, instrumentalities, officials
and entities controlled by the Government of North Korea and the
Worker's Party of Korea.

Executive Order 13687 represented a significant broadening of
Treasury's authority to increase financial pressure on the DPRK
and to further isolate it from the international financial system.
For the first time, Treasury has the authority to designate individuals and entities based solely on their status as officials, agencies,
or controlled entities of the Government of the DPRK. Treasury
also now has the authority to designate those providing material
support to the Government of the DPRK.

Simultaneous to the issue of this Executive order, Treasury designated three entities and ten individuals, whom Secretary Jack
Lew described as ''critical North Korean operatives.'' These include
the Reconnaissance General Bureau, known as RGB, which is the
DPRK's primary intelligence organization, which is responsible for
many of its cyber operations; the Korean Mining Development
Trading Corporation, also known as KOMID, which is the DPRK's
primary arms dealer; and ten officials of the DPRK Government,
including eight KOMID officials based throughout the world.

Secretary Lew also made clear that we will continue to use this
broad and powerful tool to expose the activities of North Korean
Government officials and entities. Treasury has also used existing
tools to raise the cost to the DPRK of its provocative actions.

Since 2005, Treasury has designated over 60 North Korean-re-
lated entities and individuals under Executive Order 13382, which
targets WMD proliferation-related activities, and Executive Order
13551, which targets North Korean arms sales, the procurement of
luxury goods, and illicit economic activity. Under these authorities,
Treasury has exposed and cut off access to the U.S. financial system to entities and individuals, such as the Foreign Trade Bank
and Daedong Credit Bank, which are two of North Korea's most

important banks, and have provided crucial financial support for a number of DPRK illicit activities.

We have also designated General Kim Yong Chol, the head of the RGB, whom Director James Clapper recently named as the official who likely ordered the cyber attack on Sony.

Today the DPRK is financially isolated, thanks in no small part to the actions I have described. Over the years, Treasury has ensured that the DPRK has limited access to the U.S. financial system and worked with our allies to restrict Pyongyang's access to the international financial system.

As a result of sanctions and other measures targeting the DPRK's illicit conduct, financial institutions around the world began severing their ties with the DPRK in order to avoid entanglement with North Korea's illicit activities. These actions contributed to the DPRK's economic isolation and spurs positive change in the behavior of banks across the globe.

While this increased isolation has made targeting the DPRK more complex, Treasury continues to deploy the tools at its disposal to raise the cost of the DPRK's defiant behavior and induce the government to abide by its international obligations.

The U.S. Government's response to the malicious Sony cyber attack is a demonstration of our determination to hold the DPRK responsible for its actions. But protecting the U.S. from cyberattacks isn't just about implementing sanctions, it is also about working with the private sector to safeguard our economy and the infrastructure more broadly. Beyond our response to the Sony cyber attack, safeguarding the U.S. financial system and its critical infrastructure from the threat posed by state-sponsored malicious cyber activity is also part of Treasury's mission.

Treasury partners with the financial sector to share specific threat information, improve baseline security, and enhance industry response and recovery. I go into much of this in my written testimony in greater detail.

As the United States confronts the destabilizing and destructive actions of the DPRK, Treasury is employing its authorities to isolate North Korea from the international financial system. Treasury will continue to use its arsenal of financial measures to combat the cyber threat by the DPRK.

Thank you, Mr. Chairman, for your invitation to testify before the committee today, and I look forward to answering any questions.

Chairman ROYCE. Thank you, Secretary Glaser.

[The prepared statement of Mr. Glaser follows:]

**Testimony of Assistant Secretary Daniel L. Glaser**
**House Foreign Affairs Committee**
**Confronting North Korea's Cyber Threat**
**Tuesday, January 13, 2014**

Chairman Royce, Ranking Member Engel, and distinguished members of this Committee, thank you for inviting me to speak today about the U.S. Government's efforts to counter the threat posed by the malicious cyber activities of the Democratic People's Republic of Korea (DPRK).

In my remarks today, I will describe the Department of the Treasury's financial tools related to the DPRK and how we are deploying them. I will also discuss Treasury's ongoing efforts to help support the security, resilience and stability of the U.S. financial sector.

**DPRK Sanctions**

The DPRK is a brazen and isolated regime that has repeatedly shown flagrant disregard for international law and standards. This is evident in the DPRK's development and proliferation of its illicit nuclear and ballistic missile programs, its repeated violations of United Nation Security Council resolutions, its repression of the North Korean people through serious human rights abuses, and, most recently, its cyber-attack on a U.S. company and attempts to stifle freedom of expression in our country.

In response to the DPRK's cyber-attack on Sony Pictures Entertainment (SPE) as well as numerous other egregious acts, the President signed an Executive Order (E.O. 13687) on January 2, 2015 granting Treasury the authority to impose sanctions against officials of the Government of the DPRK or the Workers' Party of Korea (WPK), as well as agencies, instrumentalities, and entities controlled by them and those acting at their direction or on their behalf. The President took this step in furtherance of the United States' commitment to hold the DPRK accountable for its destabilizing, destructive and repressive actions, particularly its efforts to undermine U.S. cyber-security and intimidate U.S. businesses and artists exercising their right of freedom of expression.

E.O. 13687 represents a significant broadening of Treasury's authority to increase financial pressure on the Government of the DPRK and to further isolate the DPRK from the international financial system. With the issuance of E.O. 13687, Treasury, for the first time, has the authority to designate individuals and entities based solely on their status as officials, agencies, instrumentalities, or controlled entities of the Government of the DPRK or the WPK. Treasury also now has the authority to designate those acting on their behalf or providing them with material support. Simultaneous to the issuance of E.O. 13687, Treasury designated three entities and ten individuals whom Treasury Secretary Jacob Lew described as "critical North Korean operatives." These included:

- The Reconnaissance General Bureau (RGB) – the DPRK's primary intelligence organization and responsible for many of its major cyber operations;

- The Korea Mining Development Trading Corporation (KOMID) – the DPRK's primary arms dealer;

- Korea Tangun Trading Corporation – the agency responsible for the procurement of technologies that support the DPRK's defense research and development programs; and

- Ten officials of the DPRK government, including eight KOMID officials based throughout the world and one Tangun official.

Secretary Lew also made it clear that "we will continue to use this broad and powerful tool to expose the activities of North Korean government officials and entities."

While Treasury's authority to target the DPRK Government was expanded significantly under E.O. 13687, Treasury has used existing tools under two other E.O.s to raise the cost to the DPRK of its provocative and illegal actions. Since 2005, Treasury has used its global WMD proliferation E.O. to designate fifty-four DPRK-related entities and individuals under E.O. 13382, which targets individuals and entities engaged in WMD proliferation-related activities. Since August 2010, Treasury has issued nine designations under E.O. 13551, which targets individuals and entities facilitating North Korean arms sales, the procurement of luxury goods, and illicit economic activities. Under these authorities, Treasury has exposed and cut off direct access to the U.S. financial system to entities and individuals such as:

- The Foreign Trade Bank (FTB) and Daedong Credit Bank: two key North Korean banks, both of which provided crucial financial support to DPRK entities responsible for a number of the DPRK's illicit activities, including KOMID;

- General Kim Yong Chol: the head of RGB whom Director of National Intelligence James Clapper recently named as the North Korean official who likely ordered the cyber-attack on SPE; and

- O Kuk Ryol: a Vice Chairman of the North Korean National Defense Commission who previously headed the WPK Operations Department, where he ordered the establishment of a nuclear research and development organization directly under his control.

I should note the importance of coordination with our international partners, particularly those in the region who share our concerns over the DPRK's destabilizing actions. Of course, we will always take the actions we deem necessary to safeguard the United States, our companies, and our financial system. We do, however, recognize that our financial measures are more powerful and effective when undertaken in a multilateral framework. This is certainly the case in the context of the DPRK, which is much more dependent on regional actors than on the United States for its economic survival. Treasury has worked hard with our partners in the region to bring greater pressure to bear on the DPRK. We have seen the fruit of this work in a number of instances of sanctions harmonization, most notably in the case of FTB, where Japan and Australia followed suit in designating FTB. Moreover, some key regional banks, including Chinese banks, severed their ties with FTB after its designation by Treasury.

Today, the DPRK government is financially isolated, thanks, in no small part, to the actions I have described above. Over the years, Treasury has ensured that the DPRK has limited access to the U.S. financial system and worked with our allies to restrict Pyongyang's access to the international financial system. As a result of sanctions and other measures targeting the DPRK's illicit conduct, financial institutions around the world began severing their ties with the DPRK in order to avoid entanglement in illicit activities. These actions contributed to the DPRK's economic isolation and spurred positive change in the behavior of banks across the international financial system. While this increased isolation has made targeting the DPRK more complex, Treasury has continued to use its sanctions authorities to ratchet up the pressure on the DRPK. For now, the DPRK remains defiant, continuing its well-documented illicit activities. As long as this is the case, Treasury will continue to deploy the tools at its disposal to raise the financial cost of such behavior and induce the government of the DPRK to abide by its international obligations. The U.S. government's response to the malicious SPE cyber-attack through E.O. 13687 is a demonstration of our determination to hold the DPRK responsible for its actions. The Treasury Department will continue to use E.O. 13687 and its other sanctions authorities to target the illicit activities of the DPRK.[1]

**Promoting the Security and Resilience of the U.S. Financial Sector**

Beyond our specific response to the SPE cyber-attack, combatting the threat posed by state-sponsored malicious cyber activity emanating from the DPRK and more broadly is one part of Treasury's broader mission to protect the U.S. financial system, including its critical infrastructure, against illicit misuse and national security threats. To safeguard the U.S. financial system from cyber threats, Treasury pursues a strategy of partnering with the financial sector to share specific threat information, improve baseline security, and enhance industry response and recovery.

In 2013, the President issued Presidential Policy Directive-21 (PPD-21) to strengthen and maintain secure, functioning, and resilient critical infrastructure across industries, and affirmed Treasury's role as the "Sector Specific Agency for Financial Services." In other words, Treasury is charged with helping ensure the security and resiliency of the financial system's infrastructure. This is a tremendous task, given that the United States has thousands of financial institutions and that finance and insurance sectors represent nearly eight percent of our annual GDP.

To most effectively achieve our objectives, robust engagement with interagency partners and the private sector is essential. Treasury chairs the Financial and Banking Information Infrastructure Committee, a standing committee of federal and state financial regulators that coordinates efforts to improve the reliability and security of the U.S. financial system. Treasury also works closely with individual firms, trade associations, and the Financial Services Sector Coordinating Council for Critical Infrastructure Protection and Homeland Security to discuss physical and cyber

---

[1] In addition to taking action to counter the threats from the DPRK directly, Treasury has also used its tools to defend the U.S. financial sector from cyber threats more broadly under both the Bank Secrecy Act and our sanctions authorities. Prominent examples include our 2013 identification of Liberty Reserve, a virtual currency system that facilitated an estimated $6 billion worth of illicit web-based activity, as a primary money laundering concern under Section 311 and our designation of two malicious Iranian cyber actors under two separate sanctions authorities just last month.

security policy. Treasury further leads the Bank Secrecy Act Advisory Group , comprised of high-level representatives from financial institutions, law enforcement agencies and regulatory authorities to ensure that the Bank Secrecy Act is being administered in the most effective and efficient way. Key topics discussed have included network security, regulatory oversight and cyber threats to the sector.

On a daily basis, Treasury promotes cybersecurity information-sharing with the financial sector and other government entities including the Department of Homeland Security. Sharing such information is critical to enhance firms' abilities to protect their networks and systems from malicious cyber activity, effectively detect and limit the impact of cyber incidents that have already occurred, and establish shared awareness of cyber threats. Treasury's Office of Critical Infrastructure Protection and Compliance Policy (OCIP), in coordination with Treasury's Office of Intelligence and Analysis and interagency partners, identifies, declassifies, and shares timely and actionable information, including threat indicators, to the financial services sector through OCIP's Financial Sector Cyber Intelligence Group.

Treasury's Financial Crimes Enforcement Network (FinCEN), as the administrator of the Bank Secrecy Act, also plays an important role in receiving, analyzing, and sharing information with the private sector related to cyber activity. Based on the financial intelligence that it receives from financial institutions, FinCEN issues advisories to financial institutions, which can help to deter illicit cyber activity and provide information useful to law enforcement. Just last month, based on financial intelligence gathered, FinCEN issued a non-public report to inform financial institutions of the risks associated with Tor networks and to assist them in their efforts to combat cybercrime affecting the sector, such as the malicious use of darknets.

**Conclusion**

As the United States confronts the destabilizing and destructive actions of the DPRK, Treasury is employing its authorities to isolate North Korea from the international financial system. Treasury will continue to use its arsenal of financial measures to combat the cyber threat posed by the DPRK.

Chairman ROYCE. General?

## STATEMENT OF BRIGADIER GENERAL GREGORY J. TOUHILL, USAF, RETIRED, DEPUTY ASSISTANT SECRETARY FOR CYBERSECURITY OPERATIONS AND PROGRAMS, U.S. DEPARTMENT OF HOMELAND SECURITY

General TOUHILL. Thank you very much, Mr. Chairman.

And Ranking Member Engel and distinguished members of the committee, thank you very much for having me today.

I appreciate the opportunity to appear before you today alongside my colleagues from the Departments of State and Treasury.

The Department of Homeland Security leads the national effort to secure Federal civilian networks, and coordinates the overall national effort to protect critical infrastructure and enhance cybersecurity. The DHS cybersecurity mission includes analysis, warning, information sharing, vulnerability reduction, mitigation, and aid to national recovery efforts for critical infrastructure information systems. DHS ensures maximum coordination and partnership with Federal and private sector stakeholders while working to safeguard the public's privacy, confidentiality, civil rights and civil liberties.

Within DHS, the office of Cybersecurity and Communications focuses on managing risk to the communications and information technology infrastructures and the sectors that depend upon them, as well as enabling timely response and recovery to incidents affecting critical infrastructure and government systems.

Our office executes its mission by supporting 24x7 information sharing, analysis and incident response for private and public sector partners. We provide tools and capabilities to strengthen the security of Federal civilian executive branch networks, and engage in strategic level coordination with private sector organizations on cybersecurity and communications issues.

DHS offers capabilities and services to assist Federal agencies and stakeholders based upon their cybersecurity status and requirements. The department engages its stakeholders through a variety of mechanisms, including information-sharing forums as well as through the National Cybersecurity and Communications Integration Center, which we call the NCCIC. The NCCIC, a 24x7 cyber situational awareness, incident response and management center, is a national nexus of cyber and communications integration for the Federal Government, the intelligence community, and law enforcement.

Our activities include, first, incident response. And during—or following a cybersecurity incident, DHS may provide response capabilities that can aid in mitigation and recovery. Through our integration center, DHS further disseminates information on potential or active cybersecurity threats to public and private sector partners. And when requested by an affected stakeholder, DHS provides incident response through the United States Computer Emergency Readiness Team, commonly referred to as the US–CERT, or the Industrial Control Systems-Cyber Emergency Response Team, commonly referred to as the ICS–CERT.

Our second activity is assessing security posture and recommending improvements. And upon request, DHS conducts risk and vulnerability assessments to identify potential risks to specific operational networks, systems and applications, and then we provide recommendations for mitigation.

Our third activity is providing technical assistance. DHS may provide direct technical assistance upon request. For instance, following attacks on the financial services sector in 2013 and 2014, our United States Computer Emergency Readiness Team went onsite with major financial institutions and other critical infrastructures to provide direct technical assistance.

US–CERT's technical assistance and technical data include identifying 600,000 distributed denial-of-service-related IP addresses, and contextual information about the source of the attacks, the identity of the attacker, and associated details behind the attack. We have had a long-term, consistent threat engagement discussion with the Department of the Treasury, the FBI and private sector partners in the financial services sector.

Regarding the Sony Pictures Entertainment incident, in November 2014, the NCCIC was made aware of a specific significant breach in the private sector, impacting Sony Pictures Entertainment. Cyber threat actors targeting Sony used a sophisticated worm to conduct cyber exploitation activities.

Since that time, DHS has initiated a series of proactive steps designed to protect not only the dot gov space from any potential spillover, but to share information with our private sector partners. We have worked extensively with our partners, including the FBI and other agencies, and international partners to share information and collaborate on incident analysis. DHS has published multiple products related to this incident, has shared with other Federal agencies, our international partners, the private sector and the general public.

As a trusted information-sharing partner to the private sector, the NCCIC does not have a regulatory role. Our mission includes securing critical infrastructure and protecting the Federal dot gov space.

As we conclude, evolving and sophisticated cyber threats present a challenge to the cybersecurity of the Nation's critical infrastructure and its civilian government systems. DHS remains committed to reducing risks of Federal agencies and critical infrastructure. We will continue to leverage our partnerships inside and outside of government to enhance the security and resilience of our networks, while incorporating privacy and civil liberties safeguards into all aspects of our work.

Thank you again for the opportunity to provide this information, and I look forward to your questions.

Chairman ROYCE. Thank you very much, General.

[The prepared statement of General Touhill follows:]

Oral Statement


Brigadier General Gregory J. Touhill, USAF, Retired

Deputy Assistant Secretary for Cybersecurity Operations and Programs

U.S. Department of Homeland Security


Before the

U.S. House of Representatives

Committee on Foreign Affairs


Regarding

The North Korean Threat: Nuclear, Missiles and Cyber


January 13, 2015

## Introduction

Chairman Royce, Ranking Member Engel, and distinguished

members of the Committee, I appreciate the opportunity to appear before

you today alongside my colleagues from the Departments of State and

Treasury.

## Roles and Responsibilities

DHS leads the national effort to secure Federal civilian networks

and coordinates the overall national effort to protect critical

infrastructure and enhance cybersecurity. The DHS cybersecurity

mission includes analysis, warning, information sharing, vulnerability

reduction, mitigation, and aid to national recovery efforts for critical

infrastructure information systems.

DHS ensures maximum coordination and partnership with Federal

and private sector stakeholders while working to safeguard the public's

privacy, confidentiality, civil rights and civil liberties. Within DHS, the

Office of Cybersecurity and Communications (CS&C) focuses on

managing risk to the communications and information technology infrastructures and the sectors that depend upon them, as well as enabling timely response and recovery to incidents affecting critical infrastructure and government systems.

CS&C executes its mission by supporting 24x7 information sharing, analysis, and incident response for private and public sector partners. We provide tools and capabilities to strengthen the security of Federal civilian executive branch networks, and engage in strategic level coordination with private sector organizations on cybersecurity and communications issues.

## DHS Services

DHS offers capabilities and services to assist Federal agencies and stakeholders based upon their cybersecurity status and requirements. The Department engages its stakeholders through a variety of mechanisms including information sharing forums as well as through the National Cybersecurity and Communications Integration Center (NCCIC). The NCCIC, a 24x7 cyber situational awareness, incident response, and management center, is a national nexus of cyber and communications integration for the Federal Government, intelligence community, and law enforcement. NCCIC activities include:

1. **Incident response:** During or following a cybersecurity incident, DHS may provide response capabilities that can aid in mitigation and recovery. Through the NCCIC, DHS further disseminates information on potential or active cybersecurity threats to public and private sector partners. When requested by an affected stakeholder, DHS provides incident response through the United States Computer Emergency Readiness Team or the Industrial Control Systems-Cyber Emergency Response Team.

2. **Assessing security posture and recommending improvements:** Upon request, DHS conducts Risk and Vulnerability Assessments to identify potential risks to specific operational networks, systems, and applications, and then to recommend mitigation.

3. **Providing technical assistance:** DHS may provide direct technical assistance upon request. For instance, following attacks on the financial services sector in 2013 and 2014, US-CERT went on-site with major financial institutions and other critical

infrastructure to provide technical assistance. US-CERT's technical data and assistance included identifying 600,000 DDoS related IP addresses and contextual information about the source of the attacks, the identity of the attacker, or associated details. We have had long-term, consistent threat engagements with the Department of Treasury, the FBI, and private sector partners in the Financial Services Sector.

**Sony Pictures Entertainment**

In November 2014, the NCCIC was made aware of a significant breach in the private sector impacting Sony Pictures Entertainment (SPE). Cyber threat actors targeting SPE used a sophisticated worm to conduct cyber exploitation activities. Since that time, DHS has initiated a series of proactive steps designed to protect the .gov space from any potential spillover. We have worked extensively with our partners, including the FBI and other agencies and international partners, to share information and collaborate on incident analysis. DHS has published multiple products related to this incident, shared with other Federal agencies, international partners, the private sector, and the general public. As a trusted information sharing partner to the private sector, the NCCIC does not have a regulatory role. Our mission includes securing critical infrastructure and protecting the dot gov.

## Conclusion

Evolving and sophisticated cyber threats present a challenge to the cybersecurity of the Nation's critical infrastructure and its civilian government systems. DHS remains committed to reducing risks to Federal agencies and critical infrastructure. We will continue to leverage our partnerships inside and outside of government to enhance the security and resilience of our networks while incorporating privacy and civil liberties safeguards into all aspects of our work. Thank you again for the opportunity to provide this information, and I look forward to your questions.

Chairman ROYCE. I was going to start with a question of Assistant Secretary Glaser. And Ambassador Kim made the point that increasingly Russia has stepped in where China has curtailed with respect to support for North Korea. He is speaking about the issue of forgiving debt and certainly the investments from Russia into the rail network. I have traveled in North Korea, and the functioning rail network just ends at the border, and once you are in North Korea, it is not operational, so—or at least none that I could see. And so the investment would seem to be critical coming from Russia.

The question I have is, is that investment that—would then be sanctionable, right? Under the interpretation that I just read.

And on top of that, if we look at the Section 311 sanctions, which you were at the center of in 2005, I remember working with you on that at the time with respect to Banco Delta Asia, there is a lot more that we could be doing here if we were to label North Korea a primary money laundering concern, as we have done with Iran. That would be possible. After all, we caught them, you know, with 100 dollar U.S. currency. We saw that in Macau, we had $100 bills there that were counterfeited out of North Korea.

So the question I have, then, is let's go to that issue of financial sanctions on North Korea. As Kurt Campbell, former top State Department official for Asia noted recently, we could really move effectively with that and make life much more difficult for those who are making life difficult in South Korea and here.

Mr. GLASER. Thank you for the question, Chairman Royce.

I certainly agree with you. It is our goal and it has been our strategy, it has been our strategy at the Treasury Department for many years now to implement sanctions and other financial measures in a way that isolates North Korea from the international financial system, and that would be from the international financial system everywhere, whether it is China or Russia or the United States or Europe or other places in Asia. The goal is to squeeze them financially as much as possible.

With respect to the new Executive order that you make reference to and that I discussed in my testimony, that is an important new tool that we have at our disposal precisely because it gives us a tremendous amount of flexibility in how we approach targeting.

So we could go—we could target any North Korean Government agency, we could target any North Korean Government official, and then once they are targeted, we could apply sanctions with respect to any individual or entity who is providing them in turn material support or any individual entity that they in turn control. So that gives us—that gives us a large——

Chairman ROYCE. And I think that is where we need to have the focus, because the Foreign Trade Bank, that was a designation a long time coming, but just designating North Korean institutions is not going to curtail the kind of hard currency that the regime uses in order to continue to expand their ICBM program, for example.

Mr. GLASER. Right. And that is why what we are trying to do is identity what their notes are into the international financial system. You mentioned Banco Delta Asia, a designation under 311 that we did 10 years ago. Why that was so successful was not with respect to the specific action on Banco Delta Asia, but that tied up about $25 million of North—money that North Korea said  was North Korean money.

But the real impact of Banco Delta Asia and that designation and that action was it that it created a chilling effect throughout the financial system. Banks around the world stopped doing business with North Korea. We still live in that world today. That action and a lot of other actions we have taken have made it a lot harder.

Chairman ROYCE. And that is why Mr. Engel and I have our legislation that we have over in the Senate, because my observation at the time was that, as you said, it wasn't just Banco Delta Asia, it was a dozen banks all that were willingly doing business in laundering, basically, or doing business with North Korea, and once those accounts were frozen, not only could he not pay his generals, but I later talked to defectors who had worked—one had worked on the mission program. He said, that program came to a halt because we did not have the hard currency. We couldn't even buy the clandestine gyroscopes that we would buy on the black market for those missiles. We couldn't pay for anything.

And that is the kind of pressure, I think, could cause a regime to recalibrate its thinking. There has to be consequences directly and it has to impact, you know, the family itself that run that country. And the best way I can think of doing that is to not give them the hard currency, so that those generals are not paid, the army is not paid. And at some point people turn and say there has to be a better way forward than the kind of repression that is going on.

And that is why we are trying to jump-start this beyond just sanctions within North Korea, to the financial sanctions that would truly, truly create additional pressure.

Do you think our legislation, which we had passed into the Senate last year, if we get that out of the Senate this year, do you think that would be a useful tool?

Mr. GLASER. Well, we, you know, you say, Chairman, that it was dozens of banks. It was more than dozens of banks; it was hundreds of banks making the decision at the time to not do business with North Korea. So we have that impact, and that is an impact that we are still—that we are—that is a world that we are still living in.

So, again, you say the goal is to identify financial institutions outside of North Korea that provide these points of access, and that is exactly what we are trying to do. You mentioned, Chairman, Foreign Trade Bank. I thought that was an extremely significant action. That was North Korea's primary source of access to the international financial system, and action——

Chairman ROYCE. True enough, but I would just point out, there are a number of small banks that we have been following that are doing business with North Korea that, frankly, if we really wanted to squeeze, we could cut that off. And if we do cut that off, it becomes very problematic for them to get the resources even to send these hackers, you know, to Moscow, or in the past they sent them to Beijing to get the kind of training. I mean, if you cut off the hard currency, these regimes like North Korea cannot carry out the kinds of offensive attacks that they are given to.

Mr. GLASER. Right. And that is exactly what we are trying to do. Foreign Trade Bank, Daedong Credit Bank, Daesong Bank, Bank of Eastland, these are banks that we have targeted with sanctions.

We used Section 311 on Banco Delta Asia. You know, the actions that we have taken have caused a chilling effect even within the Chinese financial system, even banks, major commercial banks within China have cut off their relationships with entities such as Foreign Trade Bank.

So I think, Chairman, that that is exactly the right approach that we should be taking.

Chairman ROYCE. We are on the right road, we just want to accelerate it. Dan, thanks for being here to testify today.

Mr. GLASER. Thank you.

Chairman ROYCE. We go now to Mr. Engel.

Mr. ENGEL. Thank you, Mr. Chairman.

The chairman mentioned, and I agree, that the bottom line is that there needs to be an impact on the family that runs the county, the Kim family, obviously, and all of their entanglements.

When we went to Pyongyang, now granted—I was there twice, and granted, you are limited to what you can see, we were told that we could only be in the capital, that we couldn't go outside of the capital, and then we got up early and we observed people going to work in the morning, everything seemed really normal. People looked to me like they were fed properly, people were wearing dress clothes for work, it seemed like almost any other major city, but we are told that Pyongyang is essentially where the elites live. And so the elites are treated relatively well, while the rest of the country is starving, and that is really the problem.

So what can be done to bolster the enforcement of existing sanctions in a way that would impose meaningful costs for the North Korean elites? What do we—what other levers would we have to influence them to make sure that it is not a situation of where you have elites in the capital doing relatively well, and then we impose sanctions, the sanctions hurt all the people that are starving all around the country, but the elites basically are untouched? What might we do to make sure that they are caught up in this, that they suffer the penalties for their actions?

Mr. GLASER. Thank you for the question, Congressman. I don't think that the misery that has been inflicted on the North Korean people can be attributed to sanctions. I think the North Korean Government bears sole responsibility for the misery of the North Korean people.

But I do take your point that the goal is to try to put pressure on the elites, and I think that it is precisely through access to the international financial system that we can do that, because that is who benefits, that is how the elites acquire the hard currency that the chairman talked about, the luxury goods, the other things that make their life—that make their life pleasant and that make, you know, the system run as far as the system actually runs. So that is what we are trying to do.

We are trying to identify their sources of currency. One of the important sources, for example, is conventional arms sales. That is why we targeted eight KOMID officials in our recent round of sanctions a couple of weeks ago. These are individuals who operate in places like Africa, who are raising hard currency for the regime, and we are trying to cut that off as a source.

And as the chairman said, we try to identify their points of access so that they can't repatriate the funds or they can't use the funds that they do have. We have identified a number of banks, but this is an ongoing effort. This is an effort that has been ongoing for 10 years. It is a hard target, because their needs are relatively small. They only need a handful of points of access. It makes it very effective when we do find a node. When we can put our finger on a node, we could have a big impact.

But they try to gain access through deceptive financial measures, they try to gain access through countries in which we have less influence, and so it is an ongoing effort and we are continuing to work on that. And I think that the recent Executive order gives us the flexibility to really step that up.

Mr. ENGEL. Thank you.

I am wondering if any of you can talk about the—obviously North Korea is gaining additional conventional and nuclear capabilities, and obviously it seems to us that this emboldens themselves with respect to belligerent activity in other domains, such as cyberspace.

Can anybody talk about that? I would be interested in hearing your perspective on that.

Ambassador?

Ambassador KIM. Thank you, Ranking Member Engel.

We are obviously deeply concerned about North Korea's efforts to improve their dangerous capabilities in the nuclear front, missiles, as well as now cyberspace. They pose a great threat, not just to the region, but to the United States directly.

I think what we need to do is continue to strengthen our efforts on sanctions, pressure, but also continue to work on strengthening our deterrent capability on all fronts, and this requires a continuing effort with our partners, not just in the Six-Party process, but more broadly in the international community.

I can assure you that despite North Korea's continued efforts to improve their capabilities, we are fully capable of defending against any threat posed by the North Koreans.

And I point to one upcoming example, which is our military exercise with the South Korean's that is going to be coming up shortly. This is a very important exercise, defense oriented, but very effective exercise in making sure that we maintain the strongest possible combined deterrent capability on the peninsula so that we are prepared to deal with any threat posed by North Korea.

Mr. ENGEL. And don't the North Korean's usually react hostilely to joint maneuvers between South Korea and the United States? I mean, we are saying that this drill, the joint drill that we are doing together, is routine and it is not related to a report that North Korea is trying to increase its submarine capabilities.

Whether it is or isn't, aren't we likely to see some acting out by North Korea as a result of these joint maneuvers?

Ambassador KIM. Sir, I mean, I don't want to speculate on what the North Korean's may be planning to do. You are quite correct that they don't like our exercises, because I think they understand that our exercises strengthen our combined deterrent capability. But these are routine, non-provocative defense oriented exercises that we have carried out for 40 years. We have been quite open about it. So the North Koreans really have no right to complain about these exercises.

Mr. ENGEL. Now, you mentioned, Ambassador, the Six-Party Talks. When we were there, and it was several years ago, so things may have changed, the North Koreans seemed to be more interested in having Two-Party Talks with the United States rather than the Six-Party Talks. Is that still what we—what we find coming from them?

Ambassador KIM. Unfortunately at the moment, the North Koreans don't seem to be interested in any constructive dialogue with anybody, including the United States, as well as the Six-Party Talks. I mean, we believe that the Six-Party Talks framework still provides a viable forum for discussing this issue.

One of the main reasons is that the north—it is in the Six-Party process that the North Koreans made the most clear commitment to denuclearization. It is their own commitment, and I think we need to hold them to it. And the Six-Party process also includes all of the key countries in the region that have a stake in this issue. This is not an issue just for the United States. This is an issue for the whole region.

And we have the Chinese, who actually chair the process, the Japanese, South Koreans and the Russians in the process. And I think we need to try to work within the process to make some lasting progress in denuclearization.

Mr. ENGEL. Thank you.

My last question, Mr. Glaser, I want to just follow up on the elites discussion that we had before. We find that the elites in North Korea find creative ways around the existing sanctions, obviously. They work through Chinese banks, and those banks are not exposed or integrated into the international market.

So what are we doing to go after these types of institutions?

Mr. GLASER. Well, the Chinese financial system is integrated into the international financial system. I think one good example of our ability to impact behavior even within China was, as I had the exchange with Chairman Royce, our designation of Foreign Trade Bank, which is North Korea's main commercial bank, it is the bank through which they do most of their commercial conduct.

Upon our designation, the main—the major commercial banks in China, the big commercial banks acted as you would expect any international commercial bank to act, and they announced that they were cutting Foreign Trade Bank off from their banks. So we can have an impact on commercial banks in China.

That said, I think that you are exactly right. China does provide North Korea the lion's share of its access to the international financial system. It is an issue. It is a subject that I have had discussions with the Chinese many times on, and it is something that we need to continue to talk to the Chinese about to try to get Chinese assistance in making sure that their financial system does not provide North Korea the opportunity to engage in proliferation or any other illicit economic activity.

Sung and I were talking about this just before this hearing, and I know that Sung plans on having this conversation with the Chinese as well. So it is a significant issue, and it is one we are focused on and will continue to be focused on.

Chairman ROYCE. And we will be in Beijing in March, all right, so we will continue that dialogue.

We are going to Mr. Steve Chabot of Ohio.

Mr. CHABOT. Thank you, Mr. Chairman, and thank you for convening this briefing to examine the North Korean threat.

This committee has long recognized the dangers of Pyongyang's growing capabilities. In fact, last year as the former chairman of the Asia-Pacific Subcommittee, I held two hearings specifically on North Korea because not only is it the greatest security threat to the peace and stability of Asia, but it is one of the United States' most vexing security challenges and, I would argue, greatest policy failures in many ways. So just a couple of questions.

Ambassador Kim, in June of last year, the Asia-Pacific Subcommittee heard testimony from your predecessor, Ambassador Glyn Davies, and in his testimony, he stated that China is North Korea's ''last remaining patron''; however, as Chairman Royce already mentioned, Pyongyang has a growing relationship with Russia and illicit networks with countries in the Middle East, especially Iran.

We know that North Korea maintains a fairly robust illicit trading network with these various Nation states and terrorist organizations, and last year signed an economic trade deal with Russia. This will provide Pyongyang with an economic boost to counter sanctions and counterbalance the Chinese, who have been putting some pressure on them.

In light of North Korea's recent cyber attack on Sony, there is a growing speculation about how big North Korea's cyber army really is and where it has received the training to orchestrate such an attack.

Ambassador Kim and General Touhill, could you, either of you, discuss first, who are North Korea's primary patrons at this time, and second, could you discuss where North Korea's gaining its cyber capabilities and expertise, and finally, do you have a more accurate sense as to how big North Korea's cyber army really is? And I will let either one of you go first.

Ambassador KIM. Thank you very much, Representative Chabot. I will defer to General Touhill on the cyberspace issue.

With regard to North Korea's patrons, frankly, I think North Koreans are running out of friends. I think they are becoming increasingly isolated because of their misbehavior on the nuclear front, on missiles, human rights abuses.

Of course, China has a special relationship with North Korea. They have considerable leverage over North Korea. I think what we have seen in our cooperation with China is that China is working with us more effectively in trying to stifle North Korea's dangerous activities. And it is an ongoing effort. I think all of us need to do more, including China.

Russia, as you mentioned, sir, there has been some contact, there has been some senior level discussion, some investment flows, but I believe the bottom line is that the Russians remain committed to the shared goal of denuclearization and they do want to work with us to make sure that the North Koreans move in that direction, despite some of the contact that we have seen recently.

Mr. CHABOT. General Touhill.

General TOUHILL. Thank you very much for the question, sir.

You know, regarding the acquisition of tools and capabilities in cyberspace and being able to employ them, many of these tools, as a matter of fact, most of these tools are readily available to anybody around the world through open source acquisition. Many of the tactics, techniques and procedures used by attackers in cyberspace, and predominantly criminals, are openly available through the marketplace and frequently posted online. So the acquisition of capabilities is readily available to anybody, including the North Koreans, through open source activities.

Mr. CHABOT. Thank you.

I think I have time for one more question.

I will direct this to you as well, General.

North Korea's cyber capabilities were first revealed back in March 2013 as South Korean financial services and media firms were attacked. At that time, it was it latest attack to emerge from a malware development project called Operation Troy, which revealed Pyongyang was attempting to spy on and disrupt South Korea's military and government activities.

Could you say whether North Korea's focus on using the master boot record wipe functionality, if you are familiar with that, for its attack on South Korea is similar to the attack launched on Sony, and what possible responses or protections do we have against this type of cyber attack?

General TOUHILL. Well, thank you very much for that question.

The attack using a wiper virus or capability to attack the master boot record in essence means that every computer has an instruction set that is contained in part of the disk called the master boot record, and it tells the computer what to do when it is turned on and it tells where the information is stored and the like.

Using an attack against that master boot record basically wipes out the record, and the computer no longer knows how to turn itself on and look for the information, so it is a very devastating attack to the computer.

As we take a look at the code, and we have done some malware forensics with the malicious code that was discovered as a result of this attack, it was a very sophisticated, well organized piece of code that was specifically engineered to attack that master boot record.

When it comes to detecting that type of malicious code, it is very difficult to do that for each and every piece of code. Our current database of malicious software numbers over 100 million different sample sizes.

That said, we have taken the information we have done from our malware forensics and we have loaded those indicators not only into the Einstein system to help protect our Federal systems, but we have also shared that with our international partners, with the private sector and the like.

So the indicators that we have derived from our analysis, we have shared, but this is very, very well crafted code, sir.

Mr. CHABOT. Thank you very much.

Yield back.

Chairman ROYCE. We go now to Mr. Brad Sherman of California.

Mr. SHERMAN. The witnesses should relax for a few minutes, as I have kind of an opening statement that I will use some of my time with, but don't relax too long. I will have a question for you, General, in a few minutes.

Obviously North Korea is worthy of sanctions, but how do you have trade sanctions against a nation where we have no trade, deny visitor visas to a country that sends us no visitors, name and shame a country that is shameless?

The ranking member and the chairman have pointed out that we could have secondary sanctions. Their bill does just that. And secondary sanctions are where we threaten another country or a bank or other company in another country with sanctions if they do business with North Korea, but if we are going to designate those who provide material support to the DPRK, we would start with the Government of China, which doesn't just do business with North Korea, but gives them free money, free oil, subsidies.

And I know the Ambassador points out that the Chinese have perhaps on occasion stifled North Korean behavior by pushing them to be a little bit less aggressive, but the fact is that just last month they threatened to blow up multiplexes in the districts of every member up here, so I am not sure that they have been all that stifled.

I don't think China—China has made a strategic decision: For now, regardless of the annoyances, they are backing North Korea. Every day they are giving them free oil, every day they are supporting them militarily and diplomatically.

And so we would have to do things that China disagrees with, do things to Chinese companies, do things to China's own trade relationship. One thing we could do is designate them a currency manipulator if they don't radically change their behavior toward the Korean Peninsula. This has the additional advantage of being true. They are a currency manipulator.

Since we are probably unwilling to do that, we will target this or that Chinese company or bank, I think with some success, to at least suppress and annoy North Korea, but China seems to have made a strategic decision that North Korea's success is so important, that they will give them free money, so I can't imagine that they will allow us to completely shut off their banking relationships.

So I support all the efforts of the gentlemen here and of the ranking member and the chairman to try to turn the spigot down a little bit, but I don't think we can turn it off.

There is one other thing we can do. First, we ought to reflect that this was a unique attack. It wasn't just an attack on a company, it was an attack against freedom of speech in the United States, and so I would like to give North Korea a double dose of free speech. We spend $8 million broadcasting into North Korea. We could increase that to 16. That is an additional cost of $8 million, or roughly one-thousandth of 1 percent of what we spent on the naval, air and land forces that confront North Korea.

44

Right now we are broadcasting into North Korea only 11 hours a day. The target is 12 hours a day. It ought to be 24 hours a day. And I believe that those broadcasts will undermine the regime, both with the people and the elite. I can't think of anything we can do for $8 million that would better express our dedication to the First Amendment and to posing difficulties for the North Korean regime.

I would like to explore satellite television broadcasting into North Korea, another broad television broadcasting, because I particularly want to broadcast a particular movie, and I hope that we do the director's cut before they toned down the climactic scene.

I commend to all of those on the committee the December 8th report, just a month old, issued by the Broadcasting Board of Governors, which of course oversees Voice of America and Radio Free Asia. This report was issued pursuant to the North Korean Human Rights Reauthorization Act that went through this committee.

General.

General TOUHILL. Yes, sir.

Mr. SHERMAN. How certain are you, and I realize now you are out of government so you may not have seen all the information, that North Korea is the entity that both hacked Sony and threatened terrorist action on our—against our movie theaters?

General TOUHILL. Well, thank you very much for the question, sir. Just for clarification. I just changed uniforms. I am still part of the government.

Mr. SHERMAN. Oh.

General TOUHILL. I retired from active duty and was recruited to come on board with DHS as the deputy assistant secretary for cybersecurity.

Mr. SHERMAN. Thank you for that clarification.

General TOUHILL. Thank you. Attribution of these type of events is not a function of my organization. It is a function of the intelligence and law enforcement communities. That said, I am very well familiar with the attribution methodology, the preservation of evidence, and the things that are done by the intelligence and the law enforcement communities, and based upon what I have seen and in consultation with my partners from both the intelligence communities and law enforcement communities, in this particular instance, I have—I have trust and confidence in their conclusions.

Mr. SHERMAN. And you have seen more than some of these outside experts on 24-hour news channels that think they can second guess the FBI?

General TOUHILL. Yes, sir. I have seen more than some of my colleagues in the private sector.

Mr. SHERMAN. Thank you. I yield back.

Chairman ROYCE. Thank you. We go to Mr. Mike McCaul.

Mr. MCCAUL. I thank the chairman.

Chairman ROYCE. By the way, our chairman of the Homeland Security.

Mr. MCCAUL. I appreciate you mentioning me here. Thank you. We just passed a bill the last day of the last Congress, 5 cyber security bills, one codifying, General, as you know, the NCIC, which is like the cyber command within DHS, giving you the congressional seal of approval. I see it as really the civilian portal to the private sector.

When Sony happened, I had asked the question, well, which of the 16 critical infrastructures does this fall under, and it is a bit—it is not clear. I know the President is announcing a cyber plan this afternoon. I just got off the phone with the Secretary. I think the vision is to make the Department of Homeland Security the portal civilian interface to the private sector between the Federal Government and the private sector, sharing information from various data points, whether it be NSA, FBI through the NCIC to the private sector with liability protections to incentivize participation in this civilian interface safe harbor, if you will, within the Department.

I just wanted to—and after this I want to talk about the foreign affairs aspect of cyber and the cyber jihad threat to CENTCOM that we just recently saw, but how do you view the role of NCIC of DHS broadening with respect to an event that happened with Sony?

General TOUHILL. Well, thank you very much, sir, for the question, and thank you very much for your leadership in helping us with the legislation that just passed and your continued support of the Department. Thank you very much.

As we take a look at the NCIC, integration is part of our name with the National Cybersecurity and Communications Integration Center, and as you mentioned, sir, you know, the law enforcement partners, the intelligence community, the other departments and agencies, and our private sector partners are all coming together as part of the NCIC team.

On the floor of the NCIC, which I had the honor to direct on an acting basis from August through last month, the NCIC has the ability where we are bringing in folks from all aspects of our critical infrastructure, law enforcement, and the intelligence community, as well as representatives from the Department of Defense so that we are sharing information. We are very transparent with each other.

The information ranges from top secret, sensitive compartmented information, down to unclassified information. And we are finding that these partnerships and having everybody co-located and working together is helping strengthen not only our situational awareness, but in getting solutions to issues as they come in.

We are working together to secure and make our infrastructure more resilient by leveraging the activities of the NCIC. We have come a long way in the last couple of years, and as we look to the future, the legislation that is proposed and the activities that have already occurred are making us better able and capable.

Mr. McCAUL. Well, the vision I would like to see is it expands not just to the 16 critical infrastructures but really to the private sector so the Sonys of the world could participate in this as well, and I think that is the vision. And I—personally, I like the idea of the privacy groups came out so strongly in support of not only my legislation, but also your efforts, sir, at DHS because there is a robust privacy office at the Department of Homeland Security.

I want to just close with, you know, we had the Sony attack and then we had yesterday an attack by cyber jihadists purporting to be on behalf of ISIS at CENTCOM saying, ''American soldiers, we are coming. Watch your back. ISIS.'' This is disturbing because, as a threat, vectors develop, as we look at China, Russia, the normal ones, but Iran, becoming more sophisticated, and now with these jihadist groups that we have seen attempting to get this type of technology and this type of malware, now actually be successful at hacking into our CENTCOM, into our military, ISIS, this is severely disturbing to me.

We don't know how to respond to these things. We don't—proportional response, what does that mean? Act of warfare, what does that mean?

And Mr. Chairman, I would like to work with you on a cyber agenda on this committee because it is outside the lanes of my committee in terms of what we do with other countries. Do we have a NATO alliance with cyber, one of the countries hit the other? What is the appropriate response when a nation state hits our infrastructures, and in this case, when a terrorist organization hits our military? General.

General TOUHILL. Well, thank you very much, sir. To address the points. The first one about the attack and the attribution that it got into the CENTCOM networks. First of all, this was a commercial space, a Twitter account. It didn't—there was no compromise and there is no evidence of any penetration into government and specifically the military computer systems. Rather, it was a commercially-facing bulletin board, as it were, through the Twitter account, and certainly anytime there is a compromise of any account, it is serious business. And in talking with my partners in the Department of Defense and the FBI last night, they are investigating it with all due vigor, and I will be getting an update from them later today.

Mr. MCCAUL. Just let me close with that, I think, Mr. Chairman, we have an opportunity to work in this committee on legislation that could deal with defining what is proportionate response, how other countries should respond with us, what is going to be the response of the United States of America when our companies are attacked and when our departments are attacked and when our military is under fire? And with that, I yield back.

Chairman ROYCE. Thank you. By the way, Mr. McCaul, I would be happy to work with you. I was working with Mike Rogers on a piece of legislation, and maybe we can work together on cybersecurity, and I appreciate you bringing it up and look forward to working with Mr. Engel as well on those concepts, okay.

We now go to Gerry Connolly from Virginia.

Mr. CONNOLLY. Thank you, Mr. Chairman. And Mr. McCaul, if you are looking for a Democrat, I will be glad to work with you on that as well.

Chairman ROYCE. Balance in all things.

Mr. CONNOLLY. Cybersecurity is a really big issue in my district. We do a lot of work on it, so I would be delighted to help in any way, and I thank the chairman and ranking member for holding this hearing, and welcome to our panel.

Your last comment, General, I think underscores something, though. I mean, the distinction between the private sector and the public sector when it comes to cybersecurity really isn't a helpful distinction. Eighty-five percent of the critical infrastructure in this country, for example, is controlled by the private sector. That doesn't mean we don't have a public sector interest in it, and the interface between social media and other things we may be doing in the public sector is often almost seamless and—because they are so connected.

So that is why, it seems to me, we have got to be concerned even with the kind of attack that occurred the other day on social media and the Pentagon and better understand where the boundaries are, or even if we want to recognize there are boundaries. And I think Mr. McCaul was pointing out, too, we really need to be rethinking the codification of cybersecurity attacks and the severity and what it means from our point of view, not only U.S. law but, frankly, what it should mean in international law.

When—you know, if you have a cyber Pearl Harbor, is that an act of war? I mean, at what point does the intensity and severity and magnitude constitute an aggressive act that has to be addressed?

General TOUHILL. Thank you, sir, for that question, and the magnitude and severity of the rubric of crossing that line, when does it become an act of war, is one that has been hotly and actively debated for many years.

Currently, the administration is working to put together a codified construct for the priorities and the prioritization and taking a look at it from a risk management and consequence management standpoint. That is still a work in progress, but ultimately, through our congressional processes and our constitutional processes, rather, you know, we will be making those determinations.

Mr. CONNOLLY. Right. I fully appreciate that is going to be a work in progress, but I think one of the tasks our Government faces and the international community faces is looking afresh at the legal codification of this subject because we are really at a very early stage, and I think that is—we want to make the international law serve as a tool and an ally in protecting.

I am going to try to do this real quickly. Mr. Ambassador, does my memory serve me well that a few years ago probably the North Koreans helped shut down much of the banking system in South Korea for a day or two?

Ambassador KIM. Instead there was a cyber attack on South Korean financial system.

Mr. CONNOLLY. And do we believe that was generated by the North?

Ambassador KIM. We believe so. More importantly, the South Korean authorities have indicated——

Mr. CONNOLLY. Yes.

Ambassador KIM [continuing]. That it was.

Mr. CONNOLLY. And that was—I mean, think about it, virtually the entire banking system went down.

Ambassador KIM. I don't recall the exact extent, but it was a serious attack on the——

Mr. CONNOLLY. And the South Korean economy, for example, ranks where in the world?

Ambassador KIM. 10th or 11th.

Mr. CONNOLLY. Yeah. So the 10th or 11th largest economy in the world had its banking system shut down by a cyber attack, and I think that is a real warning in terms of both what the North's capability is and the vulnerability of a whole sector of not just South Korea's economy, but, frankly, our own as well.

China. How—how helpful do we think—you mentioned in your opening statement that China has been more forthcoming and we want them to be even more forthcoming, but the Chinese themselves are engaged in cybersecurity attacks in a very systematic way sponsored by the PLA. That is state-sponsored cybersecurity attacks, so how reliable do we think the Chinese are going to be in trying to rein in the North Koreans in their cybersecurity malfeasance?

Ambassador KIM. Well, I will defer to General Touhill for part of the question.

Mr. CONNOLLY. Who are you—to whom?

Ambassador KIM. To our DHS colleague——

Mr. CONNOLLY. Okay.

Ambassador KIM [continuing]. For part of your question.

Mr. CONNOLLY. All right.

Ambassador KIM. Just more generally, I do believe that the Chinese cooperation on the North Korean issue, all dimensions of it, has improved in recent years. I would point to their cooperation in the U.N. Security Council for passing a resolution act of the North Korean nuclear test last year as an example of how their cooperation has improved. I think it can improve much further, and we are going to continue to work on persuading the Chinese that when they think about their strategic interests, unconditionally defending North Korean behavior——

Mr. CONNOLLY. Yes, but my question—we are limited in time, Mr. Ambassador. I understand all of that in general, but when it comes to this topic, cybersecurity, their hands are dirty.

Ambassador KIM. Well——

Mr. CONNOLLY. And the question, why would we count on them to help us rein in North Korean cybersecurity attacks when they are engaged in it with all four paws in the snow?

Ambassador KIM. Well, I think one of the reasons is that when they saw our company, Sony Pictures Entertainment attacked like this in such a disruptive manner, it should have been a wake-up call to Chinese.

Mr. CONNOLLY. Yes.

Ambassador KIM. The Chinese contingencies are also subject to irresponsible attacks from countries like North Korea and——

Mr. CONNOLLY. I am sorry. We are running out of time, but thank you. General, did you want to comment?

General TOUHILL. As we take a look at information sharing and the common threats and vulnerabilities that are out there, when we have a common threat, and as the Ambassador had mentioned, some of the things that were observed could just as easily threaten the Chinese, so it is in everyone's best interest to address the issues and make sure that everyone is a responsible member of the world community.

Mr. CONNOLLY. Well, Mr. Chairman, just a final observation. That sounds very noble and Boy Scout-like, but the fact is that the Chinese have been stealing military secrets from us, including weapons designs and bypassing, you know, the R&D stage for quite

49

some time in a very systematic way. The Pentagon knows that because the Pentagon has been one of the biggest victims, and it just seems to me, I wouldn't rely on the Chinese in that respect on this subject given their record, and it is a problematic aspect of what we are talking about today. Thank you, Mr. Chairman.

Chairman ROYCE. We go to Judge Poe of Texas.

Mr. POE. Thank you, Mr. Chairman. Thank you all for being here. Globally, there seems to be, among the many bad folks in the world, three main countries. You got Syria, you got Iran, and you got North Korea. I call them the SIK axis, S–I–K axis, because they are in different parts of the world, and they are a little sick. But I understand that the official definition of nuclear weapons from our Government is you have the bomb but you also have a delivery system. I want to divide that definition and just talk about the weapon, the bomb itself.

Does North Korea have a bomb of some magnitude? Ambassador? It is just yes or no.

Ambassador KIM. I wish I could just give you a simple yes-or-no answer.

Mr. POE. Can you say yes or no? I just need a yes or no. Either they have got it or they don't have it.

Ambassador KIM. Well, we know that they have continued to work on their nuclear capabilities.

Mr. POE. We all know that. Do they have the bomb, Ambassador? I just need an answer.

Ambassador KIM. I am not sure I can say that.

Mr. POE. Mr. Glaser, you got an answer?

Mr. GLASER. I would defer to the State Department on that.

Mr. POE. So you don't know whether they have a bomb or not.

Mr. GLASER. As Ambassador Kim stated, North Korea has—well, North Korea has conducted nuclear tests.

Mr. POE. And they have sent satellites into orbit.

Mr. GLASER. They have conducted nuclear tests.

Mr. POE. All right. General, you going to pick a horse and ride it? Do they have a bomb or do they not have a bomb?

General TOUHILL. Sir, I do not know.

Mr. POE. You don't know. All right.

Now, I personally think they have the capability to make one based on hearings we have had in this committee. Looking on the other end, the delivery system. The President of North Korea said he wants to develop intercontinental ballistic missiles, and for some reason, he said he wants the first intercontinental missile to go to Austin, Texas. I take that a little personally, since I am from Texas.

What is the status of the delivery system, if you know? General.

General TOUHILL. Sir, I do not know.

Mr. POE. Mr. Glaser?

Mr. GLASER. It is——

Mr. POE. Do you know?

Mr. GLASER [continuing]. Really not a Treasury Department issue, the status of the delivery system.

Mr. POE. How about you, Mr. Ambassador, back to you?

Ambassador KIM. Sir, we will be happy to provide you a full briefing in a classified setting on their capabilities, both on nuclear and missiles.

Mr. POE. Okay. Well, we have had some open hearings. They have the ability, I understand, to develop and make, as they call it, a scud in a bucket. Are you familiar with that, Mr. Ambassador? A missile that can go from North Korea to South Korea.

Ambassador KIM. Yes, I am. Yes.

Mr. POE. They have the capability to do that?

Ambassador KIM. Yes.

Mr. POE. All right. The United States used to have North Korea on a state sponsor of terror list, but it was removed in 2008. Based on what you know, do you think it might be a good idea to put them back on the state sponsor of terror list, Mr. Ambassador?

Ambassador KIM. Sir, there is—as you know, there is very clear criteria on designating——

Mr. POE. Do you think they should be back on the list? I am just asking another yes-or-no question.

Ambassador KIM. Sir, my personal opinion I don't think is relevant.

Mr. POE. But that is what I want to know is your personal opinion.

Ambassador KIM. There is a criteria. There is a process, sir, and we are constantly evaluating all available intelligence and information to determine whether North Korea should be designated.

Mr. POE. How long is that evaluation going to take? I mean, after all, they are hacking into our cybersecurity in the United States. I mean, do you all have a time limit on how long you are going to take?

Ambassador KIM. Sir, I understand your concern and frustration, but as a matter of law, the Secretary of State must determine that the government of that country has repeatedly provided support for acts of international terrorism, and we are in an ongoing process to determine whether North Koreans meet that criteria. If they do——

Mr. POE. Do you think that——

Ambassador KIM. If they do, we will take immediate action.

Mr. POE. Excuse me, Mr. Kim, I am reclaiming my time. Do you think that hacking into our system is an act of terror or not?

Ambassador KIM. I believe that is beyond my——

Mr. POE. So you don't have an opinion.

General, you got an opinion? You are in the military. Is that an act of terror or not? I mean, people are afraid to say it is an act of war. I am just wanting your opinion.

General TOUHILL. I think, sir, as we take a look at this, this is something that should be part of the public debate, and we should have a conversation not necessarily constrained to this particular incident, but as we take a look to the future for any cyber incidents, we should have a public conversation as our next step.

Mr. POE. That is the diplomatic version, I assume, but it seems to me that it is an act of terror. We ought to strongly consider putting North Korea, these outlaws, on state sponsor of terrorism list. I don't know why we are so timid in doing that. It seems like the right thing to do. The logical thing to do.

I hope the State Department eventually makes up their mind before more of these attacks occur against the United States. I agree with Mr. Connolly when he said that the line is very thin between an attack upon the Government of the United States and attack on private industry in the United States. That seems to me to be an act, an attack, is a terrorist attack. Anyway, I will yield back, Mr. Chairman. Thank you.

Chairman ROYCE. Very good. We go to Brian Higgins of New York. Mr. Higgins.

Mr. HIGGINS. Thank you, Mr. Chairman. The nuclear missile and cyber threat of North Korea is profound. Now, the question is how does the United States respond to North Korea's cyber attack on Sony, an attack to punish Sony for making a movie that humiliated the Supreme Leader. United States' options are very few. Counterattack to weaken North Korea's political military and economic assets, highly ineffectual. Number two, relisting North Korea as a state sponsor of terrorism with new sanctions, and that, we don't have much of an economic relationship with North Korea. That, too, would be highly ineffectual. The serious threat posed by North Korea far exceeds cyber attacks. North Korean cyber attacks, I think, are indicative of future intent. Intent backed by considerable capability.

There is only one geopolitical option equal to North Korea's threat, and that is to work with our allies, both new and old, to end North Korea's existence as an independent entity, and reunifying the Korean peninsula.

North Korea's nuclear threat. North Korea has four to 10 nuclear devices, and hundreds of short and intermediate range missiles. They have an active uranium and plutonium program, and it is not inconceivable that North Korea, in time, will have a nuclear capability to reach the United States.

The North Korean regime is a proliferation threat. A decade ago, it was helping to build a nuclear reactor in Syria, and it is a potential source of missiles and nuclear materials to rogue states, including terrorists. North Korea has a serious conventional military which is a threat, an existential threat to the region. It has a population of 25 million people, and the fourth largest army in the world. North Korea's army is two times that of South Korea with its population which is half of South Korea.

There are 28,500 American troops in South Korea. Further aggression by North Korea would bring the United States into a major costly and dangerous war. North Korea is a threat to its own people. Their crimes against humanity, crimes against their own people include extermination and murder, enslavement and forced starvation. One hundred thousand political prisoners held under horrendous conditions. North Korean cyber attacks against Sony are not new. North Korea regularly attacks South Korean banks and businesses.

Also, there is a changing view of North Korea by its neighbors and only economic sponsor. China and South Korea have changed their views. The South Korean President used to be lukewarm to talk about a unified Korea. Today, the South Korean President speaks openly of reunification and of the enormous economic benefits of that unification.

China is frustrated that North Korea ignores its request to freeze or dismantle its nuclear program. With a nuclear armed North Korea, South Korea and Japan will want or need to develop a nuclear weapons program. China increasingly is viewing North Korea as a strategic liability, not an asset. China views North Korea as a growing threat to China's stability, and China's ties to South Korea have flourished. China is South Korea's leading economic partner, and China's President regularly visits South Korea and not North Korea.

So while the discussion here is centered on cyber attacks, I think there is a large discussion that needs to take place. Your thoughts.

Ambassador KIM. Thank you, Congressman. I think you are absolutely right about China's evolving, improving relations with South Korea, and this is relevant to one of the points that one of your colleagues made earlier which is, I mean, what China's strategic perspective? I don't think we can continue to assume that unconditionally defending North Korean misbehavior is in China's strategic interest. In fact, I think there is an ongoing serious debate going on in Beijing on the future direction of their North Korean policy, and one of the reasons is because they see the future of their relationship with South Korea, a major trading relationship, huge flow of traffic, students, tourists, business people, and I think that is where the future is for China on the grand peninsula. And this is one of the reasons why we are starting to get more forthcoming cooperation from the Chinese with regards to dealing with North Korean threats and misbehavior.

Ms. ROS-LEHTINEN [presiding]. Gentleman's time is expired.

Mr. Duncan of South Carolina.

Mr. DUNCAN. Thank you, Madam Chairman. North Korea has a history of cooperation with a wide range of other rogue regimes, including Syria, Iran, and Cuba, although I don't guess it is politically correct to say Cuba is a rogue regime, but I am going to keep them on the list because I don't believe a tiger changes his stripes that quickly.

Let's make some connections. North Korea. A North Korean ship was seized by Panama in July 2013. It was found to be carrying Cuban and Soviet air weapons from Cuba. It actually sailed through the Panama Canal to Cuba, turned its transponder off, went to Havana, was loaded with aircraft parts, MiG–21s, and other aircraft and military hardware covered with sugar, taken back to the Panama canal, seized by Panama, found—discovered the weapons in the ship. Thirty-two crew members were released. The other three are still being held, I understand.

So you have got the Cuban/North Korean connection there. Let's talk about Venezuela. Venezuela is Cuba's largest and best ally in the region and especially in the post-Soviet era. Venezuela. If I look back to, I guess, December 2011, Venezuela's top diplomat in Miami was linked to an alleged cyber terrorism plot against the U.S. in collusion with Iran. There is another rogue connection with Iran, and there has been flights from Tehran to Havana to Venezuela, I believe.

So you have got Venezuela involved in cyber terrorism possibly against the United States, at least allegedly. You have got a Cuba connection with North Korea, and we have got now a North Korean cyber attack on an American company. Continues a lot of rogue nations involved in cyber terrorism and other things, so I have got to ask, Ambassador, how and to what extent is North Korea engaging with allies such as China, Russia, Iran, Syria, Cuba, and possibly maybe just by association, Venezuela, and the connection to cyber terrorism there?

Ambassador KIM. Generally speaking, we are obviously deeply concerned about North Korea's relations with some of the countries you mentioned. I mean, I don't have any specific information with regards to their cooperation in cyber attacks and cyber space, but we do know that North Koreans had relations with a number of the countries you mentioned, and it is something that we monitor very closely. The ship interdiction that you mentioned is one important example of how international cooperation can yield results on the sanctions front, and I think that is a very important point, because as the Congressman from New York mentioned, because of our limited dealings with North Korea directly, we need international cooperation to make sure that sanctions, both international and unilateral sanctions actually can be effective, and that the situation you mentioned is a perfect example of that.

Mr. DUNCAN. Okay. Treasury, are you tracking money? Is there any evidence of money going from North Korea to Iran to Cuba to Venezuela, any of these connections, are you aware of any of that?

Mr. GLASER. Yes, we spend a lot of time, obviously, working closely with the intelligence community that does—does the real tracking to try to identify North Korean financial networks wherever they might be, whether it is with the regime such as Iran or institutions in Iran, in Asia, potentially in South America.

To be honest with you, I think when it comes to trying to apply financial pressure on North Korea, we shouldn't take our eye off the ball, and the ball is Asia. That is where North Korea gets its primary access to the international financial system. Asia broadly, certainly China specifically, and that is—as we divide strategies to try to put pressure on North Korea, that is——

Mr. DUNCAN. They are sending some of that money in his hemisphere. They purchase weapons from Cuba.

Mr. GLASER. And we responded, I mean, as Ambassador Kim——

Mr. DUNCAN. I don't think Castro just gave them the weapons.

Mr. GLASER. Right. And that is—and again, that is why we look at KOMID, their primary arms dealer. There is other arms dealers we targeted. We are trying to go after those arms dealers. We are trying to go after the financial networks that support those arms dealers. Tanchon is the designated entity. That is the financial arm of KOMID. That is another entity that we go after.

So what we are trying to do is make it more difficult, if not impossible, I don't know that you ever get to impossible, but certainly to disrupt and dismantle their ability to move these funds around the world and ultimately repatriate and use those funds. And that involves, as you point out, chasing the financial networks, but I think importantly what it involves is identifying where the financial nodes are that allows them to ultimately use those funds.

Mr. DUNCAN. Okay. I am going to reclaim my time because you are aware of it, and I think you have answered the question for me. I want to ask on the cyber side. Are you——

Ms. ROS-LEHTINEN. Gentleman's times is expired. Thank you, Mr. Duncan.

Mr. Lowenthal is recognized.

Mr. LOWENTHAL. Thank you, Madam Chair. I am going to follow up on some questions that have already been asked, and I think to Ambassador Kim. You have already indicated that we are beginning to see indications that China, too, has grown weary of North Korea aggression. I think you answered that. I would like to know is there anything else that you could add—two questions. Is there anything else you can add to the evolving relationship that you haven't described between People's Republic of China and Pyongyang, and specifically also, what I am interested in as we go forward, how is the United States engaging the People's Republic of China and our common interests in a more stable Korea? What specifically are we doing as we go forward?

Ambassador KIM. Thank you very much, Congressman. I think in terms of evolving relations between Beijing and Pyongyang, to me it is clear that Chinese are thinking much more seriously about their North Korea policy, and I think they are beginning to realize that when North Koreans misbehave, it hurts China's own interest. It is not a question of North Koreans misbehaving without any effect on China. China's own interests are harmed when North Koreans misbehave, and I think that affects Chinese approach in North Korea, affects their cooperation with us on how to deal with the threat posed by North Korea.

One obvious example is if you look at the interaction between the leadership of China, South Korea, North Korea. Xi Jinping and Park Guen-hye have had numerous meetings in the first 2 years of their leadership. President Xi visited South Korea. President Park's second overseas visit after her election was to China after visiting the United States first, and a number of interactions in multilateral 4 as well. Zero interaction between Xi Jinping and Kim Jong Un. I think that actually says quite a bit about the state of relations between China and North Korea.

I think we want to want to work with China so that they work more effective with us, they cooperate better with us in terms of sanctions enforcement, in terms of preventing North Korea from taking provocative actions, and also in terms of working toward a credible return to negotiations, because we haven't given up on negotiations. We do want to try to resolve the nuclear issue through the Six-Party process, and I think Chinese have a clear stake in that. For one thing, they chaired the Six-Party process.

So we—this is a prominent topic between us and the Chinese at all levels. President Obama talks about it with President Xi at every meeting and on down, Secretary Kerry, et cetera, and this is an effort that will continue to take very seriously.

Mr. LOWENTHAL. Thank you. My next question is to General Touhill. You have indicated to us that you are fairly satisfied that it really was the North Koreans in terms of the Sony cyber attack even though you are not able to discuss with us some of the classified—potentially classified information.

Recently FBI Director James Comey, in responding to some of the same issues, has urged the intelligence community to declassify more details of the evidence to counter some of these skeptics. Can any of you—can you specifically talk to us about the status of declassification and whether we will be able to—what those discussions are and will we be able to see some of this information?

General TOUHILL. Thank you very much for the question, sir. Regarding that particular declassification effort, I am not part of that conversation, but overall, our position has always been information sharing requires as transparent information transfer and declassification as much as possible. We believe that it is important to share information across the whole community as much as possible, so we are very much in favor of Director Comey's efforts.

Mr. LOWENTHAL. The other question, the last question for any of you. Is there a potential fear on the part of the Chinese or others that there could be a collapse in the North Korean Government?

Ambassador KIM. I mean, I think we think about—prepare for all contingencies on the peninsula. I don't think any of us have a magic insight into what might happen to the North Korean Government any time soon, but the important thing is that we continue to coordinate very closely with partners in the region, including China, so that we are best prepared—effectively prepared for whatever happens on the peninsula.

Mr. LOWENTHAL. Anyone else wish to take—General?

General TOUHILL. I have nothing further to answer.

Ms. ROS-LEHTINEN. Gentleman's time is expired.

Mr. LOWENTHAL. I yield back.

Ms. ROS-LEHTINEN. Thank you. And now we are so pleased to recognize Mr. Ribble of Wisconsin, a new member of our committee.

Mr. RIBBLE. Thank you, Madam Chair, and I want to thank the panel. You guys have been patient this morning. Thanks for being here.

Mr. Glaser, how large is North Korea's GDP?

Mr. GLASER. I am sorry, Congressman. I don't have the exact number. It is relatively small certainly for a country that size, but we can get you the percentage.

Mr. RIBBLE. Okay. Mr. Kim, do you know, by any chance?

Ambassador KIM. Not offhand.

Mr. RIBBLE. Okay. I mean, reports—reports would tell us it is somewhere in the range of 13 to 20 billion, somewhere in that. Does that sound reasonable to you? I want to go back to the line of questioning given that about 25 percent of their GDP is agriculture. It is really relatively small.

Give you a point of reference. Sony pictures' annual revenue is 8 billion. So if their GDP is at the lower end of that spectrum, you remove the amount for agriculture, Sony's revenue is about the same size of their GDP, so this goes back to the money.

I think ultimately if you can follow the money, you can get some sense of what their capabilities actually are. I am curious again on the money, where it is coming from, and could you talk to us a little bit about the use of forced labor in North Korea, and is that part of where the money is coming from, at least the workforce is coming from?

Mr. GLASER. Well, as far as their access to hard currency, there is a little bit of legitimate trade that they engage in with a variety of countries. They also receive a significant amount of support from

China, and then, of course, they engage in a variety of illicit activity to supplement their income.

As you point out, they are a very small country. They really only care about the needs of the top echelons of their society. So by engaging in illicit activity and illicit financial activity, by engaging in conventional arm sales, they can raise hard currency that keeps things comfortable, at least for the small—you know, the small group of people that is on top.

That is why—you know, that presents us challenges and opportunities. The challenges are, they don't need broad access. When you are dealing with a country, say, like Iran and you look at our sanctions program with respect to Iran, it was a target-rich environment, and the idea was, you know, this is a large economy. We need to shut off broad access.

We have already—you know, as I had the exchange with Chairman Royce, that has already been accomplished with North Korea based on actions that we have taken in the past and just based on the fact that they are—that they self-impose isolation on themselves. So the idea is trying to identify the nodes that you could put your finger on that really have an impact. Foreign Trade Bank, Daedong Bank, Daesong bank, these are points of access to the financial system, and then how do you work with—where will they get, you know, their key points of access, namely China, to persuade the Chinese that it is in Chinese interest.

There has been a lot of questions on how do we—you know, why would China work with us? China is not going to do us any favors. China is going to work with us because it is precisely in their interest that North Korea not engage in illicit activity because it is precisely in their interest that North Korea not abuse their financial system, and we have seen their commercial banks make that decision time and again.

So that is the challenge. That is the strategy. It is frustrating because it is difficult, but it is something that we have been committed to for 10 years, and it is something that we are committed to continue in.

Mr. RIBBLE. And it is extraordinarily frustrating because the economy is so small. It is difficult to get it. That is why my question went more on forced labor and human trafficking, the element of revenue that is there because free labor is actually a large—could be a large number, and are you aware of the North Koreans using, in essence, forced labor to do construction or anything?

Mr. GLASER. Sure. You know, North Korea is a human rights disaster, and as I said before, the North Korean Government bears full responsibility for all the misery that they inflict on their people. I would defer to Ambassador Kim to get into the details of how—of the precise mechanisms by which they oppress their people but certainly there have been extensive reports on the use of forced labor.

Mr. RIBBLE. Ambassador Kim, would you would like to add anything?

Ambassador KIM. Thank you. I would just add that we know that forced labor is a part of North Korean human rights abuse. We don't have any figures on how much that contributes to their GDP, but the important thing is that the North Korean human rights record is among the worst, if not the worst, and this is why we need to pay attention to this issue, and this is why I think what happened in the U.N. Context last year is so significant with both the Commission of Inquiry report findings as well as the overwhelming passage of the human rights resolutions.

Mr. RIBBLE. Thank you, Madam Chair. I yield back.

Chairman ROYCE [presiding]. And Mr. Ribble, there has been some good reporting on the use, for example, in forestry and other sectors, mining. But forestry, in particular, the use of chain gangs, North Korean, what would you call it, forced labor, in order to bring hard currency back into the country and the fact that those workers never see any of that money.

We now go to Ms. Tulsi Gabbard of Hawaii.

Ms. GABBARD. Thank you very much, Mr. Chairman. Thank you, gentlemen, for being here. Mr. Ambassador, it is good to see you again. As you know, and as is very apparent to all of my constituents, I come from Hawaii, which is a place geographically most closest to the Korean peninsula and a place where people, people who are not sitting in rooms like this, actually monitor and listen when North Korea beats its drums and delivers its threats, and when we learn about these nuclear tests and continual increased capabilities by North Korea because it is something that is real for everyday families in Hawaii who currently sit within range of North Korea's missile program.

I think it has been unfortunate that we have seen a disconnect in a lot of different ways. Some people within our Government, others who are so-called experts on North Korea who have really been very dismissive of the real threat that exists coming from North Korea, so I appreciate that we are having this hearing to kick off this year because it is a threat that we have to take seriously.

My first question goes to Ambassador Kim and Mr. Glaser with regards to China. Clearly, China has expressed that it is in their best interest to continue to have stability, and it is good to see that they are interested in working with us to deal with the instability that is caused by North Korea's cycle of threats, and I am wondering what specific things, what specific targets are you looking for in working with China to deal with North Korea?

Ambassador KIM. Thank you very much, Congresswoman. China obviously values stability on the peninsula, but as you suggest, I think they are beginning to realize that North Korean misbehavior causes instability on the peninsula, and that hurts China's interest.

We are looking to improve our cooperation with China on several fronts. Number 1, on sanctions enforcement, and here I think we have seen some instances where Chinese enforcement has been strengthened considerably. We also want to work with them to make sure that North Koreans don't take any provocative actions, and over the years we have seen numerous examples of North Koreans taking irresponsible provocative actions; this cyber attack on Sony is just the latest example. But they have had attacks on South Korean assets, islands, et cetera. So we need to prevent North Koreans from acting that way.

We also want to work with the Chinese on how we can get back to some credible and meaningful negotiations on denuclearization because we cannot forget that the North Koreans are continuing to pursue this dangerous program, and we need to work with China and other parties in the region to try to get this problem under control and work toward lasting, verifiable, and complete denuclearization of the Korean peninsula.

Ms. GABBARD. Anything to add?

Mr. GLASER. Just to go back to your question about the types of targets that we look for and that we work with the Chinese on. I guess you could think about it this way, that there are—the North Koreans, I would say, have two primary ways that they would access the international financial system, including the Chinese financial system, and that would be directly through their banks or that would be working through front companies or individuals who are disguised—disguise their true employer, their true origin. And so we would—we would want to, we do focus on both. We work with the Chinese on both. We try to share information on both with respect to financial institutions.

As I said before, we have imposed sanctions on the major North Korean financial institutions that give it access to the financial systems, including Korea Kwan Sang Bank which has a branch in China, and this is obviously an issue that we raise on a regular basis with the Chinese. We have seen that there has been an impact, and the major Chinese banks have cut these institutions off.

Now, there are many smaller banks in China, so there are many opportunities for them to gain access, but at least as far as the large commercial banks, we know we have had an impact. With respect to front companies, that is an ongoing challenge. We try to share information with our Chinese counterparts on that so that they could take steps to protect their financial system. Sometimes they follow up on that, sometimes we are less successful in persuading them to follow up on that type of information.

Ms. GABBARD. Just real quick. Sorry. I am about to run out of time. You had mentioned earlier when the chairman brought up hard currency sanctions, you had said that they had the impact that was intended. The policy, in my view, wasn't in place long enough to really have the impact that it could have to force major change within North Korea, so we would like to see how this policy will be pursued again. I am out of time.

Mr. GLASER. Again, for 10 years now we have been trying to isolate North Korea from the international financial system. We have had a lot of success in doing that. As I said before, though, the problem is that they don't need broad access. They only need a few points of access to gain—to get what they need, which again presents challenges and opportunities. The challenges are finding those points of access. The opportunities are when you do find those points of access, you can have a major impact.

So certainly the goal, the overall goal is for North Korea to act as a responsible member of the international community. We have not achieved that goal. That is an ongoing effort that is going to be not based solely on sanctions but our overall policy and all those things Ambassador Kim talked about.

But from a Treasury perspective, we are going to keep doing our part of that which is keeping the pressure on and increasing that pressure as much as possible to try to present a starker choice for the North Korean regime as possible.

Chairman ROYCE. Congresswoman, North Korea had indicated to State that they would open negotiations again. That is where the sanctions were lifted. Unfortunately it turned out they fibbed, and this has been sort of the problem with North Korea. We get a little leverage, and then they somehow manage to convince us that they are going to turn over a new leaf, the sanctions are lifted, and then after the fact, we find out they are full bore again, you know, developing toward their nuclear weapons programs. And I think the problem, at the end of the day, having talked to their former minister of propaganda who defected into China, at the end of the day, the problem is that their number one goal is to get that ICBM delivery capability for a nuclear weapon, and we should recognize that that is what is driving them, and cutting off their access of funds to do that is very much in our national interest.

Let's go to Mr. Curt Clawson of Florida.

Mr. CLAWSON. Thank you all. Excuse me. Express my appreciation to all three of you for coming here today and also your service to our country is noted, and we are very grateful for what you do.

Let's drill down a little bit on something that was mentioned earlier if you all don't mind about submarines. The research group 38 North recently reported that North Korea may have installed vertical missile launch tubes on a submarine.

Mr. Kim, does the administration concur that North Korea has installed missile launch tube capabilities on this submarine? Does the administration believe that North Korea is pursuing a sea-based nuclear strike capability? And what would the consequences of that sort of capability be for the region, for the security of our allies, and for the security of the United States? Thank you.

Ambassador KIM. Thank you, Congressman. I don't have anything to offer in terms of specifically confirming the 38 parallel report. As I said before, we are obviously deeply concerned that North Koreans are continuing to pursue many dangerous capabilities. We do know they have been interested in developing their submarine capabilities, so I would not rule anything out. But beyond that, I would be happy to arrange a classified briefing for you in which we can provide a fuller picture of our assessment of their capabilities at the moment.

Mr. CLAWSON. I appreciate that offer. I think that would be excellent. And if, with their growing nuclear capability in the region in general, what does that imply for us and for our allies, not just in submarine?

Ambassador KIM. I think it poses a grave threat to our allies in the region. It poses a grave threat to the U.S. directly, and this is why we need to intensify our effort on all aspects that we talked about this morning, which is on sanctions, making—trying our best to cut off funding for them to use on their dangerous programs, to working with our partners, and that brought in the international community to change, to borrow the chairman's words again, to change the equilibrium in North Korea so that they realize that they cannot continue to pursue their dangerous programs and hope to get out of this international isolation that they have been suffering.

One of your colleagues also mentioned earlier that the greatest threat—I believe it is Ranking Member Engel who eloquently mentioned that the greatest threat the North Koreans pose is to their own people, and I believe that is true. I mean, having visited North Korea several times myself, I have deep sympathy for the North Korean public, which has continued to suffer as a result of the leadership's bad decisions, and I think we need to try to work harder so that we are not only dealing with the dangerous nuclear and missile programs that North Koreans are continuing to pursue but also to try to improve the situation for the North Korean public which has been suffering so badly.

Mr. CLAWSON. Thank you.

Chairman ROYCE. Bill Keating from Massachusetts.

Mr. KEATING. Thank you, Mr. Chairman, and I would like to thank our witnesses for their patience and for being here. We talked a lot about the international community and how they can affect things. I am a member also of the Cybersecurity Subcommittee of the Homeland Security Committee. We realize we have to go further than just our own domestic abilities to influence the situation, and we have discussed China a great deal. But let me ask you a question about Russia.

Russia continues to supply oil to Jong Un, and recently this reports, and I think it is for the first time that Kim Jong Un has favorably acted on an invitation from Russia to attend ceremonies in May commemorating the anniversary of World War II's ending. This, to my knowledge, is the first, one of the first public international visits that he will do as a supreme leader, so if you factor in those kind of issues, what is the relationship with Russia and North Korea in the opinion of any of the witnesses that would like to comment on that?

Ambassador KIM. Thank you, Congressman. As you point out, Russia has recently had some senior level contact with North Korean officials. In fact, Kim Jong Un sent one of his top deputies to Moscow just recently. There has been some indication of Russian investment into North Korea, but I am convinced that the Russians do remain committed to our shared goal of denuclearization. In fact, if you look at the public statements that came out immediately following the senior North Korean officials visit to Moscow was all about Russia's commitment to the Six Party process, to denuclearization, and how they would strongly oppose a nuclear test by North Korea. So yes, the picture looks mixed, but I think fundamentally the Russians do remain committed to the goal of denuclearization.

Mr. KEATING. Do you think there is any possibility that North Korea did have some assistance either in the Sony attack or other attacks from other experts, and then, you know, not to deny that their sole responsibility as the instigator, but getting expertise they may not have had, could have that happened formally or even on the private side with Russia, given their expertise in this area? Are there any concerns that that might have been a factor?

General TOUHILL. Thanks for that question, sir. You know, frankly there is—there is always that possibility. At this point, however, I have not seen any intelligence that indicates that. Thank you.

Mr. KEATING. Just lastly, because we did spend a great deal of time talking about China. What other Asian communities do you feel could be useful in our efforts to deter this kind of cyber activity? What other countries could we get assistance from allying together on this cause?

General TOUHILL. Well, thank you, sir, for that question. As we have taken a look at it from the Department of Homeland Security and our information sharing, we have several different engagement organizations such as the Asian Pacific Computer Emergency Response Team, which we did, in fact, share information on, the collection of 21 different countries. We also used our International Watch and Warning Network membership and shared information out to over a dozen other countries. This really is something that has impact across many, many different countries, and we have leveraged all of our different partnerships across the international community to share information regarding this incident.

Mr. KEATING. Great. Well, thank you. I yield back, Mr. Chairman.

Chairman ROYCE. Thank you. Thank you, Bill. We go now to Dave Trott of Michigan, a new member of this committee.

Mr. TROTT. I want to thank the chairman and all of you gentlemen for being here and allowing me to ask a few questions this afternoon. The first question is to Assistant Secretary Glaser. Do you think Executive Order 13687 is sufficient to accomplish our goals?

Mr. GLASER. Again, Congressman, our goal is for North Korea to act as a responsible member of the international community, so certainly that Executive order standing alone is not—is not going to get us there. It is about all of the Executive orders, all of the financial tools we have, combined with all of the efforts that Sung and the State Department are engaged in, and even then, it is an incredibly difficult and frustrating issue. But I don't think a single action or a single Executive order is going to get us there, nor have we asserted that it would.

Mr. TROTT. Do you think our actions and Executive orders over the past 10 years have moved the ball forward or have we lost ground with respect to what we want to accomplish?

Mr. GLASER. Again, it depends on what you are referring to specifically. I think that we have been quite successful in applying financial and economic pressure on North Korea.

Mr. TROTT. You think there are fewer human rights atrocities, you think they are paying greater heed to the U.N. After 10 years or not?

Mr. GLASER. No, I don't. As I said, I don't think that we have achieved our goal of them acting responsible, absolutely not.

Mr. TROTT. So does the Executive order give you the latitude that the chairman's bill that passed in the last Congress with respect to secondary sanctions or do you feel you need more to pursue those sanctions? Because I think earlier you, I believe you spoke and you said you supported the North Korean Sanctions Enforcement Act that the chairman introduced last year. Would that be a fair statement?

Mr. GLASER. No. It is not for me to opine on that legislation at this point. What I can say is that what the new Executive order gives us is a flexibility that we haven't had before to target the North Korean Government, to target North Korean officials, and to target those, and this is to your point, that provide material support to any designated entity. That is not authority that we have had before, and that is authority that I am sure we will put to good use.

Mr. TROTT. So if this doesn't work as well as we hope, what is plan B?

Mr. GLASER. Plan B with respect to sanctions?

Mr. TROTT. What if North Korea doesn't change its bad behavior, what is plan B?

Mr. GLASER. Well, again, there is a broad policy that is trying to move North Korea in the right direction. From our perspective, we have a strategy that we have been implementing for many, many years now to try to increasingly isolate North Korea from the financial sector, and I think that we have a lot of success that we can show. I think it is one way to bring pressure to bear on precisely the people that we need to, which are the decision makers in North Korea, because they are the ones who benefit from that.

But, again, the broad goal is not to bring financial pressure on North Korea, the broad goal is to effect a change in North Korean behavior. And as you point out, we are not there, and it is incredibly frustrating and it is something that we work on every day to try to change.

Mr. TROTT. Thank you.

Ambassador, is there any expedited effort to review the criteria to designate North Korea as a State sponsor of terrorism?

Ambassador KIM. So the criteria is set by law. So what we are doing is to evaluate all of the available intelligence and information to determine whether the North Koreans meet that criteria.

Mr. TROTT. Any idea when that will be done?

Ambassador KIM. Well, it is an ongoing process, but I think as soon as we make the determination that there is credible evidence to support designation, we will move forward.

Mr. TROTT. And what problems, let's say we made an egregious error and somehow concluded that they were actually not responsible for state-sponsored terrorism, what problems would be created for us? Would they stop being as friendly and cooperative as they have been?

Ambassador KIM. So I think it is a fairly straightforward matter in which we are trying to meet the requirements of the law, which says that the Secretary of State must determine that the government of that country has repeatedly provided support for acts of international terrorism. And we are trying to determine whether the North Koreans meet that criteria, and when we do, we will move forward.

Mr. TROTT. Any idea when that will be done, again?

Ambassador KIM. Again, I think it is an ongoing process.

Mr. TROTT. Okay. Ambassador, how does South Korea view our actions and the measures we have taken, would they like us to do more?

Ambassador KIM. They have been very supportive. We have stayed in very close touch with South Korea, as well as other allies, including Japan. As I mentioned earlier, they issued a very strong condemnation of the attack on Sony and have expressed strong support for our reaction to the attack.

Mr. TROTT. Thank you.

Yield my time. Thank you.

Chairman ROYCE. Thank you.

We go now to Mr. Tom Emmer of Minnesota, a new member of the committee.

Mr. EMMER. Thank you, Chairman Royce and Ranking Member Engel, for holding this important hearing. I would also like to thank the committee staff for their work and their patience, and the distinguished panel for attending the hearing to provide us with their analysis.

Ambassador Kim, David Albright, the president of the Institute for Science and International Security, has commented that the North Korean policy of President Barack Obama's administration has been called ''strategic patience.'' And recently the President said, in response to the hacking, the Sony hacking, that the U.S. would respond ''proportionally.'' Can you define that for me and comment, if you will, on this strategic patience reference?

Ambassador KIM. Thank you, Congressman. Strategic patience, I think, has been misunderstood as our policy. It is not. It was just a description of the approach we were taking about resumption of negotiations, precisely because of some of the important lessons we have learned from our previous efforts in negotiating with the North Koreans, both in the Six-Party process, but also bilaterally earlier in the Agreed Framework days of the mid-1990s.

We wanted to make sure to take a very deliberate, cautious approach in coordination with our partners so that if and when negotiations resume we would have a much better chance, much more credible chance of actually making some lasting progress on the nuclear issue. So strategic patience just simply referred to that approach. It was not necessarily our policy per se. And I think that is where we are still, which is to say that we want to make sure that there is adequate preparation and that there is demonstration of commitment from the North Koreans to denuclearization before we return to negotiations.

Mr. EMMER. So, Mr. Ambassador, if I can then take you to the next part of my question. And I understand that the ''proportional response'' language was in response to the Sony episode, but is the administration now signaling an increase in intensity?

Ambassador KIM. I think that would be accurate. As Assistant Secretary Glaser pointed out, the new Executive order signed by the President gives us tremendous flexibility and broad authority to go after targets. As we develop information, as we meet standards of evidence, we will designate more North Korean entities, North Korean personnel, and this will make it more difficult for them to pursue their dangerous programs.

Mr. EMMER. There are so many questions, and you have been very patient for all the people that are here. And this is a new process for me, and I know that time is limited. So if you could just give me this.

Ranking Member Engel at the beginning today talked about the delicate balance of holding the North Korean leaders accountable while at the same time being mindful of the oppressed population. Can you tell me, and maybe this is a combination of Ambassador Kim and the Assistant Secretary Glaser, but how are you doing that, managing that delicate balance, and can you give us specific examples of how these supposed expanded authorities under the recent Executive order are being applied?

Mr. GLASER. Well, again, I fail to see how any actions that we have taken through our financial sanctions or other financial measures we have applied to North Korea have negatively impacted the Korean people. As I have said time and again, the misery of the Korean people is attributable entirely to the policies and decisions of the Government of North Korea.

Why we have adopted the approach that we have adopted is for a couple of different reasons, one of which is that in order for the Government of North Korea to maintain itself it needs access to hard currency, it needs access to the international financial system—not a lot, but it does need it. So when you identify——

Mr. EMMER. And the time is running out.

Mr. GLASER. I am sorry.

Mr. EMMER. So if I could claim back the time. Could you give me a specific example of how you are doing that since the Executive order?

Mr. GLASER. Well, simultaneous with the Executive order it was announced that we had employed the Executive order with respect to 3 North Korean entities and 10 North Korean individuals. Importantly, with respect to those 10 individuals, 8 of them were employees of KOMID, which is the primary conventional arms company of North Korea. One of the impacts of that, at least as it has been reported in the press, is that the Government of Namibia is considering expelling two of those individuals. Now, this is an important source of hard currency, conventional arms sales in Africa.

So, look, I am not doing a victory lap about this, but it is an example, one example, and it is going to be an ongoing effort of how we can and how we will continue to use that authority.

Mr. EMMER. Thank you very much.

Chairman ROYCE. Mr. Issa of California.

Mr. ISSA. Thank you, Mr. Chairman.

General, a couple of questions. You are familiar in the National Defense Authorization Act of late last year that applies now that it provides sanctions against anyone supporting or engaging in industrial espionage in cybersecurity. Is that correct?

General TOUHILL. Yes, sir, I am aware of that.

Mr. ISSA. Now, let me just go through quickly a couple of questions. North Korea has no independent access to the Internet. Is that correct?

General TOUHILL. That is correct.

Mr. ISSA. So they are entirely dependent on a single strand, so to speak, of IP that comes from China. Is that correct?

General TOUHILL. That is my understanding, yes, sir.

Mr. ISSA. And do you happen to know what the bandwidth of that is, if it is publicly available?

General TOUHILL. I do not know off the top of my head, sir. We can get that for you.

Mr. ISSA. For argument's sake, let's call it the equivalent of what one home has from Cox or Comcast. So they have a range of IPs provided by China as though they were being provided by Comcast here in the District of Columbia, one line coming in from China. Is that correct?

General TOUHILL. In essence, sir, that is correct.

Mr. ISSA. So two questions. First of all, do you have high confidence today that North Korea participated in the Sony espionage and/or any other espionage in the last year?

General TOUHILL. Based on the evidence that has been provided by the Intelligence Community and the law enforcement community regarding attribution, I have confidence in their conclusion, sir.

Mr. ISSA. So pursuant to the NDAA, you now have the ability to have sanctions based on that, correct? Beyond financial. I mean, sanctions are a broader term.

General TOUHILL. Agreed.

Mr. ISSA. However, the NDAA said provide sanctions against anyone supporting or engaging. Wouldn't it inherently be said that since the only way North Korea had the ability to do this was through a route provided by the People's Republic of China, that mainland China, China itself, has in fact supported espionage? Reasonable assertion by the American people. Couldn't have done it without China, China gives them the lifeline. As we know, China monitors all of its Internet transactions, it doesn't have a true open Internet per se. China, in fact, had to know what you know. Isn't that correct?

General TOUHILL. You know, at this point, sir—and thank you for that question—I do not know what China knew at the time.

Mr. ISSA. Do they know now? Have we directed to them the knowledge that we have sufficient so they know that in fact their lifeline to the Internet was, in fact, engaged in espionage, in other words, supporting industrial espionage by North Korea?

General TOUHILL. Sir, we have shared our information with the Chinese Computer Emergency Response Team, we have had telephone conversations with them as well, and we continue to exchange information regarding this incident.

Mr. ISSA. So based on that, my question, which goes to the very heart of not the sanctions on a country that is so isolated that the only thing we know for sure is that their people are at least 6 inches shorter than people in the south, in fact, since sanctions on North Korea are extreme and have not worked, because they simply do not care enough about their people to relieve their suffering, and since the Government of China now knows that their lifeline was used to conduct industrial espionage, are we and will we hold China responsible to be an active participant in preventing this in the future, or should we, in fact, this committee, consider that under the NDAA China would then, by supporting espionage, by not taking action, be in fact held accountable in the future?

General TOUHILL. I would have to defer to my colleagues for that question.

Mr. ISSA. Well, we don't have a China desk person, but, Mr. Glaser, you are close enough. Do you agree that, in fact, if another country, anywhere, provides direct support, and the Internet line is by definition direct support, that, as we like to say, they either have to be part of the solution or they are part of the problem?

Mr. GLASER. Thank you, Congressman. I wouldn't want to opine under the statute, but I could say that, at least from a Treasury Department perspective, we are fully committed to holding entities within China responsible, and we have demonstrated that we are willing to target entities within China.

Mr. ISSA. Pursuant to China, the Government of China providing a line to the Government of Korea that has been used in industrial espionage.

Mr. GLASER. Again, Congressman, I don't think I am familiar enough with the details of all the facts and intelligence on that particular line of questioning. All I can say is that we have demonstrated that with respect to the authorities that we have, that we are prepared to use them with respect to parties that need to be held accountable.

Mr. ISSA. Thank you.

Mr. Chairman——

Chairman ROYCE. It is a very good point and it is one that in dialogue with Beijing, I certainly think, Mr. Issa, should be explored, because you are right, that line obviously has been used. And I think the other consideration is the fact that some of those involved in the hacking in the past, maybe not currently, but in the past had training in Beijing, as some have training in Moscow. And so I think reminding Mr. Glaser of the necessity of discussing this with those who might enable this kind of activity is a good point for you to raise.

Go ahead. You had the floor.

Mr. ISSA. I was only sort of befuddled that the general, who now has authority over cybersecurity ultimately, in the last days of last year we transferred principal authority over cybersecurity to Homeland Security, so the General is here, he can provide Mr. Glaser with the questions and answers as to whether or not China, one, government line, two, North Korea perpetrated this, and three, the real question, which is, if that lifeline remains in effect and another attack occurs or is occurring as we speak, how do we deal with China?

Obviously, it is beyond the scope of this hearing, but I think it is an important one of will China be part of the solution actively or are we to continue basically dealing with sanctions over a country that seems almost immune to sanctions because they are almost immune to outside hard currency except when they sell conventional weapons and/or nuclear secrets and use that to gain hard currency. That is where the challenge of how do we get China as an open partner, and that is why I had that line of questioning.

And I thank you for your indulgence, Mr. Chairman.

Chairman ROYCE. Well, thank you.

We go now to Mr. Ted Yoho of Florida.

Thank you, Mr. Issa.

Mr. YOHO. Thank you, Mr. Chairman.

Gentlemen, I appreciate you being here. I want to go back to 1994. What was the original intent of the nuclear talks and the agreement? Wasn't it to get away from nuclear proliferation and get into energy production in North Korea?

Ambassador KIM. Well, it was the same purpose that we are pursuing now, which is denuclearization, to make the North Koreans abandon their nuclear program.

Mr. YOHO. So they entered into the North Korea Agreed Framework with the United States. That broke down and they kept building nuclear capabilities. At what point were there triggers or signs that we knew they weren't staying true to their mission to get away from nuclear proliferation and getting away from—or their getting into nuclear proliferation and getting away from energy production? What were those signs?

Ambassador KIM. Well, we had credible evidence, intelligence, that the North Koreans were continuing to pursue nuclear programs despite entering into this Agreed Framework arrangement with us.

Mr. YOHO. All right. I am asking you these questions because we didn't respond in a timely manner and I want to know what parallels there are between North Korea and where we are with Iran right now in the nuclear so we don't make the same mistakes. Do you see any that we need to pay attention more closely to make sure we don't make that same mistake with Iran?

Ambassador KIM. I am not in a position to comment specifically on our ongoing efforts with Iran. But I will note in the North Korea context, as we discussed earlier with the chairman, we have learned some very important lessons from our previous efforts, both the Agreed Framework, as well as the Six-Party process, and I think this is causing us to move much more deliberately and much more cautiously toward any resumption of negotiations. Because we want to make sure that when we resume negotiations, that we are going to actually achieve lasting progress and not repeat the mistakes of what we had——

Mr. YOHO. That is exactly what we have to do, and we need to learn from the past so we don't make those mistakes with Iran.

General Touhill, what is your feeling on that as far as what we have learned from our negotiations with Korea and where we are at with Iran?

General TOUHILL. Well, thank you for the question, sir. Frankly, that is out of the scope of my expertise.

Mr. YOHO. Okay. I will come back to that. I have got some other questions here. One of these goes along the line of what Mr. Issa was saying. I can't imagine North Korea being able to act alone in this. And I don't know if it is right to say, but I would see China acting as the puppeteer or North Korea being the puppet or the stooge being directed by China. Do you feel the same way in this?

General TOUHILL. Thank you very much for that question as well, sir. At this point, I don't have any indication or any information that would indicate anybody but those that have been attributed by the law enforcement community.

Mr. YOHO. All right. Let me ask, Mr. Glaser, what do feel on that?

Mr. GLASER. I don't have any information for you on the ongoing investigation, but I can say that while China and North Korea are allies, I don't think it is correct to say that everything North Korea does it does under Chinese instructions or even blessing.

Mr. YOHO. But knowing their limited ability on the Internet, they have to be working with somebody, I would think.

How about you, Ambassador Kim?

Ambassador KIM. I think that is a very important question, and that is a question that interagency, including our Intelligence Community and our experts, should be looking at very closely to determine whether the requirements of NDAA sanctions are met by virtue of the fact that the North Koreans used an IP located in China. But I agree with Danny that there is no indication that the Chinese Government or Chinese authorities knew about the attack or in any way condoned the attack on Sony.

Mr. YOHO. All right.

One last point, and this goes off to my colleague, Mr. Connolly. He was talking about what constitutes a cyber attack and at what point do we deem it an act of war, how many people need to maybe die from it or how much damage needs to happen to a country. These are things that need to be answered so that there is clear definitions of what an act of war is, because right now I see just a big gray area, nobody is willing to commit. I think it would behoove the American Government, the American people, and improve our national security if we drew some lines and said, if you cross this line, this is considered an act of war.

What are your thoughts on that, General?

General TOUHILL. Thank you for that question. Frankly, sir, that has been debated in the war colleges for many years. And as a graduate of the War College, I believe that we should have that dialogue and we should——

Mr. YOHO. I think we don't need anymore debates. I think we need to define it, because the day is coming, I mean, with what we are seeing.

How about you, Mr. Glaser?

Mr. GLASER. I am sorry, what constitutes an act of war falls well outside my area of expertise.

Mr. YOHO. I am out of time here, so I am going to have to have you submit those, if you would, to the record.

Thank you, Mr. Chairman.

Chairman ROYCE. Thank you. Thank you, Mr. Yoho.

And let me go now to Ileana Ros-Lehtinen, chairman emeritus for this committee.

Ms. ROS-LEHTINEN. Thank you so much, Mr. Chairman.

Thank you, gentlemen.

Following up on Mr. Duncan's point earlier on the North Korea-Cuba nexus, in 2014, just recently, North Korea attempted to ship from Cuba a concealed shipment of ''various components of surface-to-air missile systems and launchers, MiG–21 jet fighters, parts and engines, shell casings, rocket-propelled projectiles, and other ammunition.''

Now, our Treasury Department did penalize the North Koreans—we thank you, Mr. Glaser—but not their enablers: The Cuban regime. Why not sanction Cuba for aiding and abetting the North Koreans?

Now, this illegal shipment of military hardware, I just read a little snippet of parts of what it entailed, were traveling from Cuba to North Korea in containers filled with sugar, quickly melting sugar. Panamanian officials stopped it at the canal, and the North Korean captain attempted to commit suicide. He didn't try to commit suicide because he feared U.N. Sanctions or he feared U.S. sanctions. He feared the revenge of Kim Jong Un.

Now, I want to know why we don't sanction Cuba for aiding and abetting the North Koreans and why didn't we work with the U.N. So that the U.N. Could impose their sanctions. You correctly point out, Ambassador Kim, that sanctions are important. This is what the U.N. Response was. This is the Security Council committee four-page, strongly worded memo. That is what Cuba got. It said, the concealed cargo of arms and related materiel, illicit cargo, to include the hazardous cargo, was not declared on the ship's manifest and the cargo was hidden under 218,000 bags of raw sugar.

But, boy, they got really tough. They said, the committee encourages all member states to remain vigilant regarding their obligations and responsibility to inspect suspect cargo to prevent prohibited items going to and from the DPRK and to ensure the relevant national implementing instruments, blah, blah, blah, blah, blah. In regard, the committee draws the attention of member states to security resolution—oh, my golly.

This is all that happened, when they were shipping MiGs and everything else under melting sugar. And you talk about the sanctions and how important they are, yet the Treasury Department looked the other way. It was like that ship just came magically from Cuba, a phantom ship, violating all kinds of sanctions of the U.S. and the United Nations, and there was no penalty to pay. So we wonder why North Korea does what it is doing and why it is in cahoots with other rogue nations. So I encourage you to be a little tougher. It takes two to tango. North Korea was not shipping these on their own.

And lastly, Mr. Chairman, I know I am out of time, but on WIPO, I have been very concerned about this, and with former Ranking Member Howard Berman we asked for an investigation on the transfer of U.S. origin technology by the U.N.'s World Intellectual Property Organization (WIPO) to North Korea and Iran. And it was clear that this administration did nothing to prevent WIPO from transferring sensitive dual-use technology to North Korea and that it has not taken the threat of technology transfer seriously.

Incredibly, after WIPO Director General Francis Gurry knowingly withheld the organization's transactions with North Korea in 2012, in violation of U.N. Security Council resolutions, WIPO again ran a controversial mission to North Korea last June and has been less than forthcoming with details about that mission. Yet not only was Gurry not held accountable, he was once again reappointed, in May 2014, as director general of WIPO, with little resistance from the Obama administration. We just looked the other way.

What are we going to do to prevent U.S. technology and U.S. taxpayer dollars from being transferred in the future when we have that kind of an attitude? We don't have much time, you don't need to answer. Sanctions are important, we need to implement them. A strongly worded memo from either the Treasury or the U.N. Is not going to do the trick, it is not going to stop anybody.

Thank you, Mr. Chairman.

Chairman ROYCE. Thank you.

In adjourning here, let me thank our witnesses, but let me also say that Mr. Engel and myself look forward to working with State and Treasury. We are going to bring this legislation up again that we passed into the Senate last year, and we are going to try to move it fairly quickly. So we will be meeting with all of you.

And I think that, frankly, a lot of these actions against North Korea have been very long in coming. And for those of us that have urged a more robust response, we want to make certain the tools are there to do it, do it effectively, and cut off the hard currency for the regime. So we will be in contact with you. Thank you very much for your testimony.

[Whereupon, at 12:37 p.m., the committee was adjourned.]

# APPENDIX

---

## MATERIAL SUBMITTED FOR THE RECORD

# FULL COMMITTEE BRIEFING NOTICE
## COMMITTEE ON FOREIGN AFFAIRS
U.S. HOUSE OF REPRESENTATIVES
WASHINGTON, DC 20515-6128

**Edward R. Royce (R-CA), Chairman**

January 8, 2015

## TO: MEMBERS OF THE COMMITTEE ON FOREIGN AFFAIRS

You are respectfully requested to attend an OPEN briefing of the Committee on Foreign Affairs, to be held in Room 2172 of the Rayburn House Office Building (and available live on the Committee website at http://www.ForeignAffairs.house.gov):

**DATE:**          Tuesday, January 13, 2015

**TIME:**          10:00 a.m.

**SUBJECT:**    The North Korean Threat: Nuclear, Missiles *and* Cyber

**BRIEFERS:**    The Honorable Sung Kim
Special Representative for North Korea Policy and
Deputy Assistant Secretary for Korea and Japan
U.S. Department of State

The Honorable Daniel Glaser
Assistant Secretary for Terrorist Financing
Office of Terrorism and Financial Intelligence
U.S. Department of the Treasury

Brigadier General Gregory J. Touhill, USAF, Retired
Deputy Assistant Secretary for Cybersecurity Operations and Programs
U.S. Department of Homeland Security

### By Direction of the Chairman

*The Committee on Foreign Affairs seeks to make its facilities accessible to persons with disabilities. If you are in need of special accommodations, please call 202/225-5021 at least four business days in advance of the event, whenever practicable. Questions with regard to special accommodations in general (including availability of Committee materials in alternative formats and assistive listening devices) may be directed to the Committee.*

## COMMITTEE ON FOREIGN AFFAIRS
MINUTES OF FULL COMMITTEE BRIEFING

Day ___Tuesday___ Date ___01/13/15___ Room ___2172___

Starting Time ___10:10 a.m.___ Ending Time ___12:37 p.m.___

Recesses ___0___ (___to___)(___to___)(___to___)(___to___)(___to___)(___to___)

**Presiding Member(s)**

*Edward R. Royce, Chairman*
*Ileana Ros-Lehtinen*

*Check all of the following that apply:*

Open Session ☑
Executive (closed) Session ☐
Televised ☑

Electronically Recorded (taped) ☑
Stenographic Record ☑

**TITLE OF BRIEFING:**

*The North Korean Threat: Nuclear, Missiles and Cyber*

**COMMITTEE MEMBERS PRESENT:**

*See Attached Sheet.*

**NON-COMMITTEE MEMBERS PRESENT:**

*None.*

**BRIEFING WITNESSES: Same as meeting notice attached?** Yes ☑ No ☐
*(If "no", please list below and include title, agency, department, or organization.)*

**STATEMENTS FOR THE RECORD:** *(List any statements submitted for the record.)*

*None.*

TIME SCHEDULED TO RECONVENE _____
or
TIME ADJOURNED *12:37 p.m.*

Jean Marter, Director of Committee Operations

# HOUSE COMMITTEE ON FOREIGN AFFAIRS
*FULL COMMITTEE BRIEFING*

| PRESENT | MEMBER |
| --- | --- |
| X | Edward R. Royce, CA |
|  | Christopher H. Smith, NJ |
| X | Ileana Ros-Lehtinen, FL |
| X | Dana Rohrabacher, CA |
| X | Steve Chabot, OH |
| X | Joe Wilson, SC |
| X | Michael T. McCaul, TX |
| X | Ted Poe, TX |
| X | Matt Salmon, AZ |
| X | Darrell Issa, CA |
|  | Tom Marino, PA |
| X | Jeff Duncan, SC |
| X | Mo Brooks, AL |
|  | Paul Cook, CA |
| X | Randy Weber, TX |
| X | Scott Perry, PA |
|  | Ron DeSantis, FL |
| X | Mark Meadows, NC |
| X | Ted Yoho, FL |
| X | Curt Clawson, FL |
|  | Scott, DesJarlais, TN |
| X | Reid Ribble, WI |
| X | Dave Trott, MI |
| X | Lee Zeldin, NY |
| X | Tom Emmer, MN |

| PRESENT | MEMBER |
| --- | --- |
| X | Eliot L. Engel, NY |
| X | Brad Sherman, CA |
|  | Gregory W. Meeks, NY |
|  | Albio Sires, NJ |
| X | Gerald E. Connolly, VA |
| X | Theodore E. Deutch, FL |
| X | Brian Higgins, NY |
|  | Karen Bass, CA |
| X | William Keating, MA |
| X | David Cicilline, RI |
|  | Alan Grayson, FL |
| X | Ami Bera, CA |
| X | Alan S. Lowenthal, CA |
| X | Grace Meng, NY |
| X | Lois Frankel, FL |
| X | Tulsi Gabbard, HI |
| X | Joaquin Castro, TX |
| X | Robin Kelly, IL |
| X | Brendan Boyle, PA |
| X |  |
|  |  |